ADVENTURES IN SERVIA: OR, THE EXPERIENCES OF A MEDICAL FREE LANCE AMONG THE BASHI-BAZOUKS, ETC.; PP. 10-248

Published @ 2017 Trieste Publishing Pty Ltd

ISBN 9780649038442

Adventures in Servia: Or, The Experiences of a Medical Free Lance Among the Bashi-Bazouks, Etc.; pp. 10-248 by Dr. Alfred Wright & A. G. Farquhar-Bernard

Edited by Trieste Publishing Pty Ltd.
 Cover @ 2017

www.triestepublishing.com

DR. ALFRED WRIGHT & A. G. FARQUHAR-BERNARD

ADVENTURES IN SERVIA: OR, THE EXPERIENCES OF A MEDICAL FREE LANCE AMONG THE BASHI-BAZOUKS, ETC.; PP. 10-248

 Trieste

INCIDENT DURING RETREAT. UPSET OF AMBULANCE.

Adventures in Servia:

OR THE

EXPERIENCES OF A MEDICAL FREE LANCE AMONG THE BASHI-BAZOUKS, ETC.

By DR. ALFRED WRIGHT.

EDITED BY

A. G. FARQUHAR-BERNARD, M.R.C.S.,
Late Surgeon of the Servian Army.

WITH SIXTEEN DRAWINGS BY THE EDITOR.

LONDON:
W. SWAN SONNENSCHEIN & CO.,
PATERNOSTER SQUARE.
1884.

Printed by Hazell, Watson, and Viney, Limited, London and Aylesbury.

PREFACE.

WHEN my esteemed friend Dr. Wright asked me to edit this work and also to write its preface, I agreed to do so, but not without a considerable amount of hesitation and diffidence, for I was loth to run the risk of marring what appeared to be a very excellent book by my own necessarily imperfect workmanship.

The good doctor, however, placed the matter before me in such a light, that I felt constrained to comply with his wishes.

I cannot lay claim to the "pen of a ready writer," therefore I trust the public will excuse what may appear to them to be a halting style. And now to the real business of my preface.

I have the author's word for it that at least three out of every four of the incidents herein narrated really took place, and that to the fourth only such proportion of romantic dressing and spicery has been added as would enable it to harmonize with the rest.

Moreover, I am desired to state that every character depicted in these pages had its living prototype.

Thus Marie, Colonel Bragg, Savrimovitch, Colonel Philipovitch, the ruffian Pauloff, Dr. Ibaum, etc., represent real personages, whose names even, in some cases, have been preserved. The quarrel with Von Tummy, the upsetting of the waggon, the fight for the bed, the pig incident, the occupation of the cottage, the description of the battle, are all fairly accurately described ; and the conversations with Russian officers about India and with the Nihilists are reported almost verbatim.

Facts are stubborn and eloquent things, and I can say nothing stronger in behalf of these pages than that they treat, for the most part, of absolute facts.

My duty to Dr. Wright prohibits me from drawing this preface to a close without making some reference to the painful circumstance that my distinguished friend has as yet received no considerable token of the public favour. As he pathetically puts it, "Monarchs don't seek his medical advice, kings consult him not, and sovereigns neither summon him to their sick-bed sides, nor find their way, in another sense, into his coffers."

The doctor says he occasionally sees a person clad in prints, but never any one "en prince," and he reminds me, moreover, that though Pope lays it down as an axiom, that "what ever is, is *Wright's*," yet he gets hardly any of it at all.

Now this, I maintain, emphatically and without fear of contradiction, ought not to be, and I would respectfully intimate to the potentates of Europe, that unless they patronize the illustrious doctor more largely than they have hitherto done, there is some fear of his throwing physic to the dogs, and becoming, if not a Nihilist, at least a desperate Radical.

I state this entirely on my own responsibility. May those whom it directly concerns take it seriously to heart.

A. G. F. B.

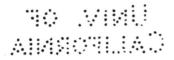

revolver apiece, and a somewhat scanty supply of clothing, which included, nevertheless, our volunteer uniforms,
each adorned with a Geneva cross on the arm, and our
preparations were complete.

The day of our departure arrived. We proudly
donned our uniforms, which, though rather the worse for
wear, still had the advantage of looking as if they had
seen service, and took our places in the train. We
intended to travel to Vienna by rail, and from thence to
Belgrade by the Danube steamer. Our journey was
uneventful, except that our uniforms attracted more
attention than was altogether pleasant.

The French mistook us for Germans, and scowled
angrily at us, and the Germans took us for Frenchmen,
and regarded us with cold hostility. In fact, wherever
we went, people seemed to wonder who on earth we were,
and what the dickens we wanted.

At Salzburg we were accosted by a stately and
elegantly-attired lady of middle age, who informed us
that she was the Princess Woronzoff, and saying that she
was delighted to see Englishmen espousing the Servian
cause, requested us to convey the sum of five Napoleons
from her to the Servian sufferers by the war.

This we promised to do, and she bade us farewell.
We arrived at Vienna late on a Friday evening, and
stayed there until Sunday morning, putting up for the
time at the Goldenes Lamm Hotel; and Hiems utilised
the time by coaching me up in the broad-sword exercise,
at which he was a proficient. He was particularly careful

to teach me the hanging guard position, and I flatter myself that I learnt it thoroughly. It certainly is a very striking attitude, and when my cap was cocked properly on one side, and I had my big boots on, I must have looked very killing.

The next morning we repaired to the steamboat quay, full of eager anticipations of what we considered would be the most interesting and picturesque part of our journey, for Strauss's favourite waltz had led us to believe that the Danube was both beautiful and blue.

We were, however, grievously sold. From Vienna to Belgrade, there is simply no scenery at all. The banks of the river are flat and dreary-looking, and the water itself is brown and dirty, so we soon turned our attention to our *compagnons de voyage*.

In the boat with us were a dozen handsome lads, all clothed alike in dark-grey tourist suits, and who seemed to be under the charge of a tall, military-looking man.

We ascertained that they were some of the King of Bavaria's pages.

These lads appeared to be greatly impressed .by our romantic uniforms and martial appearance, and presently one or two of them, who spoke English fairly well, entered into conversation with us. They were particularly curious to see our cutlasses. We showed them the weapons ; and I believe that I made a profound impression upon them, and convinced them of the invincibility of English seamen by frowning fiercely and trying to show, cutlass in hand, the hanging guard I had so recently acquired. The jealous Hiems endeavoured to dissuade me from flourishing my sword, by the remark that the young Germans would only laugh at me. I did not believe him, and am happy to say that my efforts extorted from one of my audience the acknowledgment that he thought Englishmen were very brave and hardy, and that he attributed their love of adventure to the rough nature of their sports, such as " *the* football and *the* cricket," and so forth. A corpulent little Hungarian doctor, too, watched our proceedings with great interest, and very politely proffered us each a cigar.

"Gentlemen," said he, when we had all three lit up, "is it true that you are going on the Servian side?"

"Quite true," responded Hiems, puffing vigorously at his cigar and nodding.

"And you are Englishmen, born in England?" interrogated our new friend.

"We are Englishmen, but not born in England," responded Hiems. "I was born in Ireland."

"And I in India," said I.

"An Englishman, born in India!" replied the Hungarian lifting up his eyes and hands with astonishment; "and yet you are going on the Servian side! It is amazing! It is incredible! Don't you know that the Russians are the enemies of your country, and that they want to get Constantinople?"

"I know that we fought them and beat them in the Crimea," replied I.

"Yes, and England did very well; she did right then. And what are you going on the Servian side now for? Don't you know they are the same as the Russians, and that the Russians have got up this war? Why are you not on the Turkish side?"

Hiems replied that we went as medical men, and not as combatants.

"That's worse," answered our little friend; "for as fast as the Turks knock a man over, you set him on his legs again!"

"Then again," said I, "the Servians are short of medical men."

"So much the better," said this bloodthirsty little Magyar, "the war will be over all the sooner then. No, no; you take my advice, and go over to the Turks!" His Russo-phobism did not prevent him from chatting very pleasantly with us afterwards, and he proved a most agreeable and interesting companion.

Dinner was served in the saloon at seven o'clock. Our Hungarian friend and a large party, however, did not dine then, but stationed themselves at the other end of the saloon, where I heard him telling the others that we were Englishmen.

"They are Englishmen, Englishmen!" said he, with a graceful wave of his handkerchief towards us; "and one of them was born in India. They eat a good dinner, you see. They have each had a plate of soup and a beefsteak with eggs, and some sweets, and now they will both have coffee. Ah, no! One of them, you see, has

tea——" (here he stepped quietly up and looked over
our shoulders), " and the other has coffee. Englishmen,"
he repeated, as he retired on tip-toe to his seat again ;
" Englishmen—one of them born in India—and they
have eaten a most excellent dinner ! "

When the boat stopped at Pesth our eccentric little
acquaintance went on shore; we remained some time
longer to see our luggage transferred to the Belgrade
boat, which lay alongside our own, and met him no
more.

" Five o'clock ! Belgrade in half an hour ! " such were
the sounds which, roared in a stentorian voice by the
steward, roused me from a pleasant sleep, the sixth
morning after we left Charing Cross. I was wide awake
in an instant, and dressing quickly hastened on deck ;
but a thick mist hung on the river, and Belgrade was
still invisible. The sun's rays soon, however, dissipated
the haze, and there, within a few hundred yards of us,
lay Belgrade, an imposing array of white-walled, green-
roofed buildings and churches with glittering spires,
rising terrace on terrace to a considerable height above
the water's edge. It looked so bright and beautiful that
Hiems and I were in ecstacies of delight, and congratulated each other again and again on having selected so
charming a spot for the basis of our operations. The
boat presently drew up alongside the jetty, and a tall
Servian official in a smart blue uniform with very broad
scarlet stripes down the sides of his pantaloons stepped
on board and collected all the passengers' passports.

THE HUNGARIAN GENTLEMAN TELLS HIS FRIENDS
THAT WE ARE MAKING AN UNCOMMONLY GOOD
DINNER.

To face p. 14.]

Then came a number of drowsy-looking porters, who began to overhaul the luggage and solicit patronage for the different hotels. We selected one who seemed more active and was tidier than his fellows, and instructed him to convey our things to his hotel, the " Königin von Griechenland." The man instantly summoned four or five assistants, each of whom, in an indolent and casual manner, commenced dragging one or two of our packages after him. We followed their chief up a steep flight of steps, cut in the hill or cliff on which Belgrade stands, and they followed us, droning a dismal and most unmelodious ditty in chorus. These steps were converted by a number of beggars into a kind of rag and deformity bazaar. On one of the lower steps sat a miserable creature, who, from some freak of nature, had been born without any arms; at the other end of the same step sat a blind, toothless old man, who mumbled forth a request for a piastre, and who was clad in such unsavoury garments that we felt almost plague-stricken as we passed; a little above was a frightful dwarf, a victim apparently of goitre; above him again was a man whom accident or war had deprived of both legs; then came a deaf and dumb woman; and so on right away up to the top of the steps.

The " Königin von Griechenland " was not an imposing-looking edifice; however, it seemed as good as any of the other hotels, and was fairly comfortable. We were shown into a bright, clean-looking room with two beds in it. Here we had a glorious wash and changed our linen, and then went down into the coffee-room, where some dozen persons were smoking cigarettes, drinking coffee, and playing billiards. For breakfast they brought us excellent coffee, fresh eggs, and white bread-and-butter.

Seated at the next table was a portly old priest with flowing locks and a rosy—a suspiciously rosy—face. For some time this reverend gentleman surveyed us minutely, carefully, and critically. Nothing from the top of our caps to the soles of our boots, and from our black cross-belts to the little red Geneva crosses embroidered on our arms, escaped his scrutiny. At length he rose with slow and dignified gravity, and bowed, and saying some words in a language which neither of us understood, seated himself opposite to us at our table. As he was a priest, we rose and returned his salute, and then shook our heads to betoken our ignorance of his language.

Nodding to us again, the new-comer beckoned solemnly to one of the waiters, and gave him some instructions in an undertone. Then turning to us with a smile and another nod, he said, interrogatively, "Ingleski ?" (English.) Hiems said "Ja" and I said "Oui" in our best German and French. The priestly face beamed with smiles, and then the waiter brought in three large glass flagons of foaming ale. The priest pushed one of these to Hiems, another to me, and taking the third himself, he motioned to us to drink. As we raised the glasses from the table he clinked his against ours with much cordiality and another series of smiles and nods. Then leaning back on his seat and folding his hands on his lap, he surveyed us again. At last it occurred to Hiems to try him with German ; so pulling himself together and pronouncing his words as carefully as possible, he said,—

"Sprechen Sie Deutsch, mein Herr ? "

" Ne—nein," replied the priest, shaking his head once more.

" I'm afraid it's no go," said Hiems, with a sigh ; " and it's a pity, too, for he seems an uncommonly nice old fellow. I wish we could have expressed our appreciation of his kindness better than by grinning and nodding at him."

" So do I," said I ; " but I don't see how we're to do it, except by getting him to drink with us."

Hiems reflected for a moment, then suddenly brightening up, said to me, " You know you used to be a swell at Latin at school, old chap. Try if you can't polish up some of it now. I have heard that all foreign priests talk Latin."

" That's not at all a bad idea of yours, Hiems," said I, not without a little pride. " What shall I say to him ? "

" Say—why say, ' How do you do ? ' to him, and ask him to have another drink."

" Confound it, Hiems, ask me to say something sensible. How the dickens do you expect me to translate sentences like that ? "

" What ! can't you translate them ? " asked Hiems.

" No, of course not," replied I. " The Romans never said things of that sort to one another."

" What dummies they must have been, then," replied my friend in disgust.

For a few seconds we were silent. All at once Hiems brightened up again.

" What is the Latin for ' This ' ? " said he.

" What ? " said I, not knowing what he was alluding to.

" *This*," said he again with considerable emphasis.

" Which ? " said I, quite puzzled.

" What a fellow you are ! Why *This*, the article, noun, adjective, pronoun, or whatever you like to call it. —*This*."

" Oh ah ! Now I see," said I, perceiving that he meant the word *this*. The Latin for this is Hic."

" Why could not you have said so before then ? " replied he, tartly ; " and what is the Latin for *is* ? "

" Est," rejoined I, without a moment's hesitation.

" And for ' beautiful ' ? "

" Pulcher."

" Now we are getting on," said Hiems ; " and for ' beer ' ? "

" I don't know. Call it wine, vinum."

" All right ; that will do, I suppose." Then to the priest, " Hic est pulcher vinum."

For a moment our companion was puzzled. Then his face beamed with a smile of intelligence. He nodded, grasped Hiems by the hand, and said,—

" Bibamus alterum poculum."

Then he began to speak Latin so fast and fluently that I could not catch a single word. But before the waiter could be called I was relieved from my embarrassment by the sound of martial music in the street. Every one—priest, billiard players, and ourselves—hastened to the window and looked out. A long and solemn procession was approaching—the funeral *cortége* of an officer who had been mortally wounded in the recent fighting. At the head of the column marched a military band play. ing the Servian Dead March, then twelve priests with banners and flags, a regiment with arms reversed, and last of all the coffin borne on the shoulders of eight men. The lid of the coffin, as is the custom in Servia, was removed, so that the pale face of the dead man was visible. His breast was covered with flowers; two soldiers marched behind, one bearing his sword and the other his cap. The procession slowly filed past, and when we looked round—lo! our jolly friend the priest had disappeared.

CHAPTER II.

LEFT to ourselves, we held a consultation as to what our next step should be. We both fancied that Servia was a very small country, and imagined that we were but a moderate distance from the front.

This illusion was quickly dispelled by the *maître d'hôtel*. From him we learned that the scene of action was at least one hundred miles away, also that an English officer, Colonel Bragg, who commanded a newly-raised squadron of cavalry, was then in Belgrade.

This was indeed acceptable news. His camp, we were told, was only about two miles away, at a place called Topchidere, on the other side of the town, and we determined to offer our services at once.

It was now about half-past ten o'clock, and intensely hot. There was not a cloud in the bright blue sky, and the sun's rays beat down with fierce and dazzling power on the white and dusty streets. We, therefore, fortified our muffin-shaped forage caps with puggarees, after the Indian fashion. Amongst other things I had brought out with me were a pair of india-rubber half Wellington boots, very loose about the uppers, and shiny like goloshes. I was rather proud of these, and being anxious to make a favourable impression on my distinguished fellow-countryman, I determined, in spite of Hiems' protest that they were " ridiculous," to wear them.

After a dusty walk we arrived at Topchidere. The cavalry camp, which contained only a score or two of tents, was in a large field. We had no difficulty in finding Colonel Bragg's quarters, being directed thither by a good-natured little doctor, who introduced himself to us as Dr. Ibaum, and offered us each a pinch of snuff. Our reception by the colonel was not encouraging. He was talking to a tall, good-looking young fellow, who turned out to be the special artist of an English illustrated paper, and as he approached we heard him say,—

" Who the —— are these beggars, and what the —— do they want here, I wonder ? "

The artist looked towards us, and burst out laughing. Nothing daunted, however, we walked up to the tent, and Hiems, saluting politely, said,—

" Colonel Bragg, I believe ? "

"Hulloh ! " said the colonel to his friend, "they're English ! " (*Then to us.*) " Yes, Bragg's my name. What can I do for you ? "

" We are medical students, just arrived from England, and hearing that you were organising a body of cavalry, we have come to offer you our services," said Hiems.

" D——d good of you," said the colonel, " but I don't think we want any surgeons. What stores have you got with you ? "

We replied that we had a good supply of quinine, Ipecacuanha, Condy's fluid, opium, strapping, bandages, cotton-wool, prepared oakum, lint, etc.

" Hum—well, you can send them over here, if you like, and I'll just think the matter over ; but—you were never going to the front in those idiotical boots, were you, sir ? " said he to me.

" Indeed I was, sir," said I, rather angrily, for his contemptuous tone and manner of speaking nettled me.

" More fool you, then," said the colonel.

I was so incensed at his rudeness that I turned on my heel and would have left him there and then, had he not sung out in a kinder tone,—

" Come, come, my lad, don't be riled. I'm a blunt soldier, and always speak my mind. Shake hands ; there ! " and he held out his hand with a rough good-nature that almost made amends.

" By the way, though, my lad," said he, " if you can't take a joke in good part, you'll hardly do for a campaigner ; blows are harder to bear than jokes."

" Not when you can return them, sir," replied I, haughtily.

" Well spoken," said the colonel. " So you are really anxious to go to the front ? "

" Yes," we both replied in a breath, " and we don't mind if we get a little fighting as well as doctoring," added Hiems.

" Well," said the colonel, with a fierce twirl of his moustache, " I guess you'll get a good chance of both if you come with me. I shall not forget you, only bear in mind that it will probably be two or three weeks before we shall leave for the front, for my men beat creation for stupidity at drill, and will want a lot of licking into shape before they'll be fit to face the Turks. What's your hotel?"

We told him.

" Very well, then ; you'll hear from me before we leave. Good morning;" and lighting another cigarette, the colonel turned away from us and resumed his conversation with the artist.

We left the camp, not over well pleased with our reception, and were walking moodily homewards, when we were hailed by a loud "Yai! Gospodina!" and, looking back, we beheld a soldier running after us, with a piece of paper in his hand. On taking the paper we found the following words written on it, "Dr. Ibaum make to the English gentlemen his esteem, and will say to them a few words." The soldier pointed to our right, and there was the doctor, snuff-box in one hand and hat in the other, beaming on us with the kindliest of smiles.

"Eh !" said he, "my dear friend, you have seen the Inglis camp, eh? And how love you Kol-o-nel Bragg, eh?"

We replied that we thought Colonel Bragg a first-rate soldier, but that we were disappointed to learn that he was not going to the front for two or three weeks, as we were anxious to get to work immediately.

"You will to work now, aha! Then I will say what I will do," said the little doctor, puckering up his face into a look of the most unfathomable profundity. "The Minister of the Health here, Dr. Savar Petrovitch, is great friend to me." Here he drew himself up and looked very important. "I will speak to him for you, and he shall make you some work very soon—quick—aha—eh?"

We made an effort to thank him, but he stopped us at once.

"For what," said he, "will you thank me? All Inglismen my friend; I love him. But you, you will to work for my country; why will you then to thank me? No, no, I thank you! I will now," continued he, "to walk with you some way. Will you let—eh, my Inglis friend?"

We were only too glad of his company, and the kind-hearted little man was good enough to walk back with us as far as our hotel, and when he left us, it was with a promise to call for us the next morning, and accompany us to the offices of Dr. Savar Petrovitch, the Minister of Health.

CHAPTER III.

TRUE to his promise, Dr. Ibaum called for us at ten o'clock the next morning, and accompanied us to the War Office, where we were introduced to Dr. Petrovitch.

Dr. Petrovitch received us kindly. He was a small, slightly made, but good-looking man, with dark eyes, whiskers, and moustache, and spoke French very fluently.

We informed him that we were anxious to go to the front, but he replied with a smile that they had plenty of medical men there, but were greatly in want of them at Semendria and Belgrade.

" You can choose between the two places," he said. " Belgrade is the more agreeable; there is more society there, and you won't be so dull. On the other hand, Dr. Ibaum works at Semendria, and will look after you if you go there. I have promised Baron Von Tummey, our inspector of hospitals, not to send any more surgeons to Deligrad, but to keep them for our hospitals at Semendria and Belgrade."

This was terribly disappointing, and we should probably have declined the offer, in the hope of getting to Deligrad with Colonel Bragg, but for Dr. Ibaum.

2

"Come you with me," he said, coaxingly. "You shall be glad all the tay long. You shall eat—ah! very much and good—and you shall drink—oh! you shall drink wine and beer and *café;* you shall have horse and you shall have dog; you shall have money,—oh! much money,—and you shall not work."

"That won't do for us," said I. "We want to work. We have come here for the sake of working."

"Aha!" said the little man, his eyes gleaming with satisfaction; "you will to work, you shall work then—plenty work—as much as you will to do, and you shall have money. How much money will you to have?"

We replied that we would be content with £2 per week and board and lodging.

"Yes, yes; you will to have two pound Inglis per the week—yes, that is *vier ducaten* " (four ducats). "Yes, I will speak with Dr. Petrovitch. Will you so good to wait one minute? Aha! I come quick back." And, taking Dr. Petrovitch by the arm, he left the room with him for a moment.

When they returned, Ibaum bore in his hand a couple of papers.

"Gentlemen," said Dr. Petrovitch, in French, "we are quite willing to engage you as assistant surgeons at a salary of four ducats a week; we will provide you, moreover, with board and lodging. I cannot promise that you shall go to the front, but you shall not be forgotten should an opportunity offer. Will you allow me to see your passports and certificates?"

We complied with his wish, and finding the documents satisfactory, the papers before mentioned were handed to us to sign, and we were informed that our engagement was completed.

No one perhaps was better able to revive drooping spirits than cheerful, chatty, little Dr. Ibaum. After the arrangements were made, out came the inevitable snuff-box. He insisted on our taking a pinch, then linked his arms in ours, and led us out of the room.

"Now, my dear friends," said he, looking from one to the other of us, and giving us both a gentle pat on the back, "we shall be no more grievous. If you will be sad, I will, too, to be sad, but we will not be grievous. After our work we have done, we will sing Inglis song and Servian song, and we will dance;" and suiting his actions to his words, he adopted a dancing step and broke out into a merry tra-la-la!

That evening we dined with the doctor at his hotel. He was an excellent host, and gave us a first-rate dinner *à la serbe*. We began with papricash, a kind of tomato soup. Then came caviare, fried schill, and cray-fish, then pork cutlets and beefsteaks served with potatoes and poached eggs. Portions of roast goose and roast turkey figured most conspicuously in the meat course. Then we had sweet omelettes and pancakes called palachinkas, and wound up with dessert and coffee. For drinks we had a native wine called Vaslauer, which resembled Burgundy in colour and flavour; champagne, and a spirit made from plums, called sligievitch, which had an agreeable odour, but, to my mind, a most horrible taste. After dinner the doctor waxed very jovial and communicative, " I lof," he said, " ze Englis charactaire. Ze Englismans lof horses and togs ; all Englismans lof horses and togs, and will hunt much. When I have knowed ze excellent good Englis charactaire, then have I self taught mine self ze Englis tongue, and speaks him not fine, but so also too not wicked.

Shortly afterwards our papers arrived from the War Office, and Dr. Ibaum informed us that we were to start for Semendria at six in the morning.

CHAPTER IV.

NEXT morning the doctor made his appearance with military punctuality. We breakfasted together and paid our reckoning, and left the hotel, much to the disappointment of the landlord, who doubtless had hoped that we should stay a week or two with him. Nevertheless the good man was overwhelmingly polite, and accompanied us to the top of the steps leading to the landing-place, where he remained bowing and rubbing his hands as long as we could see him.

Before embarking we had to run the gauntlet of the beggars, who displayed their deformities and mumbled for piastres with redoubled vigour as we approached. Dr. Ibaum looked at them kindly with a complacent satisfaction. He evidently regarded them as pathological curiosities, and appeared to be as proud of them as a cockney of the most famous lions of London. He stopped and spoke to a great many of them, and gave a copper or two to all.

A dirty little steamer was waiting at the quay. We went straight on board with our baggage, and as soon as we had stowed it away made ourselves comfortable in the fore part of the boat. The scenery became rather more picturesque as we left Belgrade. On the Servian side of the Danube the ground undulates, and forms a succession of slight eminences, upon one of which Belgrade is built.

Just opposite to us, on the flat Hungarian shore, was an Austrian block house, in front of which paced a sentinel, whose bayonet glittered brightly in the sun. At some distance off we saw a large town, which Dr. Ibaum told us was Semlin. The water here was anything but clear, still it was not so muddy as we had seen it higher up.

The Danube is so shallow in the greater part of its course that vessels drawing more than three or four feet of water have to proceed with the greatest caution. We were going with the stream, which was very strong, yet I don't think the boat throughout the journey ever went at a greater rate than seven or eight knots an hour, so that we were afloat nearly three hours, although the distance between Belgrade and Semendria is barely twenty miles.

However, the weather was lovely, and the air fresh and pleasant, the sun not having as yet attained its full strength. The arrival of a steamboat was evidently a remarkable event at Semendria, for the landing-place was crowded with people. The majority of them were dressed *à la Turque*, in baggy knickerbockers, jackets, and fezzes ; only a few wore European costume. Our uniforms at once made us objects of such interest, that we were followed about by a crowd, much to the delight of

Dr. Ibaum, who astonished the multitude by speaking in English. The hospital at which we were to work was a tumble-down wooden building of two stories. · It stood some twenty yards back from the roadway, and the ground in front was fenced with a rough, irregular wooden paling. In one corner of this enclosure stood a disused pig-stye, which gave forth a very disagreeable and piggish odour. The hospital was built on a most irregular plan. It jutted out here and went in there in the oddest fashion. The upper storey was reached from the outside by a rickety wooden flight of steps, which sloped into the yard. We were met as we entered the latter by Dr. Ibaum's colleague, Dr. Lazar Stephanovitch, a short, thick-set, coarse-looking man, who conducted us into one of the wards on the ground floor. This was a room some thirty feet long by fifteen wide, paved with tiles, and lighted by eight small windows, four on each side. The windows did not open, and there being no other means of ventilation than the door, the stench was terrible. The floor, too, was in a very dirty condition.

In this delightful place some twenty wounded men were lying on as many beds. Every now and then one of them would utter an exclamation of pain, but the majority of them bore their sufferings patiently, and some were even chatting cheerily. There were no female nurses in the establishment, their places being taken by soldiers chosen for the duty by lot. These men did not strike me at first sight as being suited to the work. Like most of the Servian peasantry, they were clumsy, good-natured simpletons. I saw directly that there would be plenty for us to do, and wished to set to work at once; but Dr. Stephanovitch informed me that their patients' wounds had all been dressed for the day. I pointed to the windows, and expressed my dissatisfaction at the ventilation. He replied that the building was a make-shift for a hospital, and that they were compelled to make the best they could of it. Then, after addressing a kind word or two to each patient, the doctors invited us to accompany them through the other wards, of which there were three.

Throughout the hospital I found the condition of things much the same. The men had fairly comfortable beds, and were well fed, but there was an utter want of ventilation, of cleanliness, and, as I have already stated, of properly qualified nurses. Dr. Ibaum also told me that they were very short of splints, bandages, and disinfectants, and that our supplies would be most acceptable, so we arranged to send them into the hospital that evening. Neither he nor Dr. Stephanovitch would accept the money we had collected in London, so we enclosed it in a letter, and sent it off to Dr. Petrovitch at the War Office. The two doctors informed us that they began work at the hospital at six in the morning—and usually completed their rounds by ten o'clock, after which they took it in turns to remain on duty for the rest of the day. We were requested to be there at six also, and they expected to receive in a day or two a large batch of wounded men from the front, so that we must be prepared for hard work. We had some little difficulty in finding any lodgings within a convenient distance of the hospital, and were compelled to be content with a large room in a pretty one-storied house, the front of which was overgrown with flowering creepers. The room looked clean, and had a large window which opened on to a little piece of front garden. The bed linen, we were glad to observe, was snow-white. We asked Dr. Ibaum to settle the terms, and after a little chaffering with the landlord, he arranged that we were to pay one ducat a week for board and lodging—terms which we considered astoundingly moderate, although Dr. Ibaum informed us they were very high, and explained that he had not been able to manage better for us, because the war had forced up the price of everything.

When we had secured the room, the kind little doctor invited us to accompany him to the house of a relative who was overseer of the extensive vineyard belonging to Prince Milan in the neighbourhood of Semendria, from which he acquires a considerable portion of his revenue.

After a delightful walk through an undulating and beautifully wooded country we reached the vineyard. The house of the overseer, M. Ristovitch, stood on a little eminence in the centre of the vineyard, commanding a view over a great part of the estate. Our approach, therefore, was soon perceived, and with true Servian hospitality M. Ristovitch came forth to meet us, and invited us to join his family. The party consisted of M. Ristovitch and his wife,—a comely middle-aged lady,—Mademoiselle Ristovitch,—a pretty brunette with beautiful dark eyes and luxuriant black hair,—and a Bulgarian girl, Mademoiselle Miloikovitch, taller and slighter than her companion. There was a restlessness and self-possession in the manner of this fair Bulgarian which reminded me considerably of Miss ——, the popular English burlesque actress, whose voice, too, hers much resembled.

We were soon on the most friendly terms, and odd as it may seem, our quickly-formed intimacy was in some measure attributable to the mosquitoes with which the house and vineyard swarmed. The Servian name for mosquitoes is Kamaratz, and we excited not a little amusement by calling them Karamatz, which, I believe, means elephant, or some other huge animal. From the attacks of these pests our entertainers, both ladies and gentlemen, defended us in a manner at once original and simple. While I was speaking, a mosquito settled upon my face. M. Ristovitch perceived it, and promptly succoured me by crushing the insect between his finger and my skin ; and this proceeding, which was frequently repeated, was as amusing to us as our mis-pronunciation of Kamaratz was to them—nay, more, the younger ladies especially came to our assistance so frequently, and with such bewitching grace, that they made a very deep impression upon our too susceptible hearts. Hiems was captivated by the beautiful Servian, and I was led in chains by the lovely Bulgarian. After dinner tobacco and cigarette papers were produced, and we all—ladies as well as gentlemen—fell to smoking and drinking coffee. Before leaving England I entertained a narrow-minded and bigoted objection to ladies smoking, but the charming grace with which these fair Sclav damsels put a cigarette to their pretty lips, took a little whiff, and then with an elegant turn of the wrist and play of the hand, removed it, breathing forth small puffs and wreaths of fragrant smoke, caused my prejudices to melt away.

Presently the young ladies sat down to the piano and discoursed excellent music, and Mademoiselle Miloikovitch sang a Bulgarian love song, of which I did not understand a single word,—more's the pity,—to a quaint and plaintive melody. Then, to our dismay, we were called upon to contribute to the entertainment. Hiems, who could play a little, strummed forth his stock waltz, "The Beautiful Blue Danube."

This our entertainers seemed to regard as a special compliment to them and their muddy river, and they applauded enthusiastically. Then came my turn. My treacherous friend declared that I had a superb voice, and sang exquisitely. This absolutely false statement filled me with confusion and despair. In vain did I cough and use my handkerchief, and protest that I had a frightful cold. My villainous comrade told them not to believe me, so the two ladies, particularly Mademoiselle Miloikovitch, led me firmly but gently to the piano, and fixing their lovely eyes upon me, alternately coaxed and commanded me to sing an English song. My *rèpertoire* at that time was very limited, consisting only of "God

save the Queen," and the "Perfect Cure!" I selected
the former, and sang it as well as I could to a one-finger
accompaniment, played by myself. They recognised the
air immediately, and joined us in the chorus most
harmoniously, and after it was over, were pleased to
greet my humble and discordant effort with prolonged
applause.

Emboldened by this success I was tempted to sing
the "Cure," much to their delight and amusement.
Dr. Ibaum seemed more pleased than any one else, for
he clapped his hands and shouted "Bravo! Bravissimo!"
until he was hoarse, and then went about informing
every one that these were real English songs. When he
had somewhat recovered from his excitement, he sat
down to the piano himself, and shouting out, "Dance,
dance!" he commenced playing in admirable style the
"Soldaten Lieder" waltz. At this the girls signalled to
us to help them, and we wheeled the furniture from the
centre of the room, and then . . .

Alas! the pleasantest meeting comes to an end. When
we had had a few most delicious waltzes, Dr. Ibaum
informed us that it was time to set our faces homeward
again, so we thanked our new acquaintances for their
hospitality, and prepared to bid them adieu. All insisted,
however, on accompanying us to the vineyard boundary.
Presently our revolvers became objects of interest.
Ristovitch and Ibaum expressed a desire to see their
effect upon the stump of an old tree. We readily complied with their request, but our revolvers being "Bull-

dogs," weapons that make a tremendous report, and with which it is almost impossible to hit anything, the shooting was very indifferent. Mademoiselle Ristovitch put her fingers in her ears, and gave a pretty little scream every time we fired, but Mademoiselle Miloikovitch seemed greatly interested, and presently, to my surprise, asked me to load the weapon for her, and to allow her to have a shot. I did so after some remonstrance. As I handed the pistol to her, a singular change came over her face; the fresh colour died away from her cheeks, the amiable light in her eyes was replaced by a fierce sparkle, and her lips were sternly compressed together. Taking a steady aim, she fired three successive shots at the tree, and the third time succeeded in hitting it.

Dr. Ibaum subsequently informed me that several of her relations had been massacred by the Turks in 1875, and that she herself had shot two Bashi-Bazouks in making her escape.

CHAPTER V.

BESIDES the Servian hospital to which we were
attached, there was another in Semendria, supported
by the Russian Red Cross Society, and of which all the
staff were Russians. On our return we found awaiting
us an invitation to spend the evening with the Russian
doctors, and as Ibaum was going, too, we accompanied
him. We were received with hearty courtesy, and as we
expressed a wish to see their hospital, they very kindly
took us over it. The arrangements there were as excellent as those at our place were faulty. The ventilation
was first-rate, the wards were beautifully clean, and the
air in them smelt fresh and pure. Venetian blinds to the
windows tempered the heat of the sun. There were four
wards, each of which contained about twenty wounded
men, and to each ward was a trained nurse. These
nurses, indeed, were lady medical students. When we
entered, one of these ladies was applying a bandage to a
man's arm with a skill that I have never seen surpassed.
Adjoining the hospital was the house in which Dr.
Cutemoff and the rest of the staff resided,—a long one-
storied building, with rooms of considerable size. The
evening being cool and pleasant, a table had been taken

in the garden and spread with a substantial meal. Tea, coffee, beer, wine, spirits, sardines, preserves, caviare, soda-water in syphons, jars of tobacco, books of cigarette-papers, grapes, and jugs of milk were displayed in tempting profusion. After we had all partaken of this good cheer, the tobacco and cigarette papers were handed round, and a general and cosmopolitan conversation began. Only three of the lady medicals were present, the other one remaining on duty at the hospital ; but the three who honoured us with their presence were really shining lights in their way. None of them could be called beautiful, but they all had clever and intelligent faces. The plainest of the trio, indeed, a Mademoiselle Dinah Mitykoff, struck me as being the cleverest. The conversation was carried on by different members of the company in French, German, Russian, and English, amid the clattering of glasses and clouds of tobacco smoke. This Mademoiselle Dinah Mitykoff, next to whom I was sitting, began by abruptly asking me if I was a radical.

" No," replied I, " I am a liberal conservative."

She fixed her eyes upon me (they were blue eyes, not very large, but uncommonly sharp and bright) with a somewhat contemptuous expression, and then after a short pause blew forth from her lips a cloud of cigarette smoke, which completely concealed her face for a moment, and asked me " why I was not a radical."

" Because I appreciate law and order, and dislike extreme views and measures," replied I, somewhat nettled at her contemptuous manner; "and radicalism means the subversion of order, and consists of nothing but extreme views and measures."

Again she looked at me with the same aggravating expression; then she said, "When you are older and wiser, sir, you will know that radicalism means progress."

Considering that she did not seem more than a year or two older than myself, her rebuke amused me greatly. I replied, however, that I did not admit that radicalism was synonymous with progress; on the contrary, I thought it tended to disorder and chaos, and consequently retrogression, and I added that most eminent radicals were either furious fanatics or unpractical dreamers.

"You are wrong, monsieur," said she. "We radicals are the most practical people in the world, and, for my part, unless I believed in the progress of mankind in this real and tangible world towards greater liberty, happiness, and knowledge, I should discard all faith in religion. Mark my words, the time is not far distant—nay, it is almost at hand—when kings and emperors will be swept aside, and even distinctions of nationality will cease to exist. The whole human race will live together in harmony and brotherly love, and though my country seems one of the most backward now, she will be foremost in leading to the change."

"Amen," said Dr. Knifem, one of the surgeons, in a deep voice, moving his chair closer to us. "The changes Mademoiselle Dinah Mitykoff foresees will assuredly come soon, but they will be preceded by a universal and terrible revolution—a tornado which will blow away the tyrannies and abuses that now infest and poison the world. Then, woe betide the enemies of human progress!"

"What will you do to them? Will you cut their throats?" said I, with a smile.

"Yes, like rats," said he, a fierce gleam shooting across his face.

"You are a radical, I presume?" said I.

"I am an enemy to tyrants and a friend of liberty. Call me what you like,—radical, socialist, or nihilist,—anything you please," replied he.

"But, my good sir," said I, "there are great numbers of persons who, like myself, believe themselves to be really greater friends of progress than you radicals, but who are strongly opposed to extreme measures and revolution. Are we, too, to be knocked on the head?"

"You must decide for yourself, sir, which side you take when the critical time comes, and if you choose the wrong side, you will have only yourself to thank if you suffer for it."

"And you are so convinced that your views are right, that you would make war on other nations to promulgate them."

"Yes, we would make war on tyrants," replied he.

"What!" said I, "and kill thousands of your fellow-creatures, bombard towns, and bring ruin and desolation on hundreds of happy homes?"

"I have told you already, sir, that we would even

3

make war in support of our views. I know as well as
you that war is a horrible and atrocious thing, but at
the very worst, it can only affect a fractional part of one
generation, whereas untold generations would reap permanent advantage by the triumph of our glorious cause."

"Come, come, ladies and gentlemen," said Dr. Cutemoff, "that is enough of politics for the evening. You'll
never make converts of each other by argument. I
never yet came across any one who was argued out of
his convictions. Let us have a game of cards."

CHAPTER VI.

THE next morning we were up betimes. The Servians are early risers, and the landlord and servants of the hotel were up and about before five o'clock.

Dr. Ibaum called for us,—gay and festive as ever,—and brought his English dog, Bee-lee, with him, a pretty little black-and-tan terrier.

"Aha! my friends, my friends," said he, "how you to do this early morning? Have you slip well, eh? Are you slippy steel? (Sleepy still.) No! good-good! Will you to snuff? No? So, so. Here, Bee-lee, my Inglis tog! Bee-lee! Inglis name! Ah! he come to see my Inglis friend. Inglis tog will to see Inglis man. Eh—ha! ha! ha! Beelee, say you how do now—good tog!"

Bee-lee sat up on his hind legs and held out a paw.

"Bee-lee good beggar, jolly good beggar—eh?" said the doctor complacently to us.

We were amused by the doctor's droll language and loquacity, and Hiems replied that the dog was a first-rate beggar.

"Yes," said the doctor, "I have teached him all myself, when he was small pup-dog. But come, my dear friends, now must we to the hospital go. Bee-lee shall to carry my stick, and I will take your arm." So saying, he threw his cane into the garden, when Billy rushed after it with a shrill yelp, seized it, shook it, after the manner of dogs, and finally trotted off with it— wagging his tail rejoicingly, and looking round every now and then to see if we were following him. A few minutes' walking brought us to the hospital, where we found Dr. Stephanovitch already at work. We lost no time in following his example. I was requested to attend to the out-patients. These consisted, for the most part, of men who had received slight wounds about the face or arms, also a good many malingerers, who to avoid going to the front had mutilated themselves by placing a finger over the muzzle of a rifle and pulling the trigger with the other hand. Some of these fellows had punished themselves much more severely than they had intended, and in one or two instances their hands were completely shattered, and, as might have been expected, they displayed very little fortitude whilst having their wounds dressed. As there was no special out-patients' department, I attended my cases in one of the wards, in which, at the same time, Dr. Ibaum was engaged with the in-patients, some of whose wounds were of a very painful nature. To my surprise, those who were waiting their turn laughed at the contortions of their suffering comrades as a capital joke, whilst a few minutes after, these, in their turn, would be laughing at the grimaces of the other unfortunates. The Servians are naturally a kind-hearted race, and this apparent heartlessness was due, evidently, to a keen sense of the ludicrous. I have seen Servians roll over one another in fits of laughter at a very feeble joke. The Servian doctors prized our Condy's fluid very highly. After its introduction, the mortality, so they said, was distinctly diminished, and wounds to which it was applied certainly healed up with great rapidity. The rest of our supplies also were of considerable service, particularly a large case of Liebig's Extractum Carnis. The Servians make excellent soup, but do not understand beef-tea, and many of the patients who could not take the soup on account of its greasiness, were able both to take and enjoy the former.

With the consent of Drs. Ibaum and Stephanovitch, one of the uppermost panes in each of the windows was knocked out and replaced by a small Venetian blind; and to impress our soldier nurses with the importance of cleanliness and set them an example, Hiems and I sprinkled the floor over with diluted Condy's fluid, and swept the ward out ourselves. The soldiers looked on with approving smiles, and we thought we had made a great hit. We were, however, mistaken. The next morning I found the floor of my ward untouched. Putting on a stern expression, I beckoned one of the soldiers up, handed him the broom, and motioned him to set to work with it. The man, however, impudently, amid the laughter of his comrades, returned the broom to me, and motioned to me to sweep. I was so indignant that I seized him by the collar and turned him

out of the ward, bestowing a kick upon him as soon
as I had got him outside the door. The fellow did not
mind being turned out of the ward, but objected to the
kick, and aimed a blow at me in return, whereupon I
was compelled, in self-defence, to knock him down.
I then handed him the broom once more, but he sulkily
refused to take it. I was puzzled what to do for the
moment. Suddenly a happy thought struck me. I took
the commission I had received from the War Office out
of my pocket and showed it to him. On it was the State
seal. This seemed to make a great impression upon
him. I then mentioned in succession the names of
Prince Milan, M. Ristic, and Dr. Sava Petrovitch,
looked very grave and determined, and once more
handed him the broom. The soldier took it without
a word, and set to work immediately. I then showed
the commission to the other men, and repeated the
talismanic names to them, with—I am happy to say—
the same success. After this they always behaved with
the greatest civility, and I never had occasion to complain
again of the untidiness of the ward. Hiems had some
trouble also, but Dr. Stephanovitch interfered, and
compelled the soldiers to obey him. We were very
short of splints at this hospital, and had to improvise
them out of old boxes or anything that came to hand.
We showed some of the most intelligent of the men how
to dress wounds, and in a short time they became really
zealous and useful assistants.

Stephanovitch and Ibaum worked hard and unremittingly, and we also did our best, but in spite of our utmost efforts, mortality amongst the severely wounded was very high. The Servians have an invincible repugnance to amputation, and many lives which might have been saved were lost through obstinate refusal of the men to submit to the operation. At the front the soldier's consent was not asked, but in our hospitals no operation was permitted without it. The Servian transport system—for the wounded—at that time also was extremely defective. Semendria was more than eighty miles from the scene of action, the roads were, in many parts, extremely rough, and yet scarcely any of the waggons in which the wounded were conveyed had springs. Travelling, even for those in sound health, was far from pleasant, whilst the sufferings of wounded men—with, in many instances, unset, fractured limbs, and exposed to the fierce heat of the Servian sun—must have been something almost too shocking to contemplate.

The journey from Deligrad to Semendria in these waggons occupied from two to three days. It is not surprising, then, that many of the severe cases were moribund when they reached us, whilst not a few actually died *en route.*

The work of the day at the hospital over, we used to spend our evenings in various ways. The most agreeable, perhaps, were passed with the Ristovitch family, whom we occasionally entertained at our quarters. Our landlord, a genial old Serv, on these occasions placed his whole house at our disposal, and his wife—a kind-

hearted, buxom, but withal active dame—would bustle
about the house making the necessary preparations.
After tea the young ladies gave us lessons in Servian,
whilst M. Ristovitch smoked his cigarette and looked
on, and his wife knitted, and every now and then
offered a suggestion.

How we enjoyed ourselves!

We generally had two lessons every week—one at
M. Ristovitch's house, and one at our own, and at one
of the latter we had quite a little adventure. Hiems
and I had been out for a walk. We had gone as far as
the old fort at Semendria,—a ruined castle built by the
Turks about the middle of the fifteenth century, and a very
favourite resort of ours, for we used to wander amongst
the ruins and hunt for snakes. A species of adder
abounds there which attains a considerable size, and
which the Servians hold in great dread. I have killed
them quite four feet in length. The Servians say that
the bite is fatal. On the day in question we turned
over a huge stone in our search, and in so doing dis-
closed a very fine snake. The creature gave a fierce
hiss, and endeavoured to escape, but we belaboured it
with our sticks until it appeared to be dead, and then
we took it back with us in triumph. At home it was
placed in a basin of water to cleanse it from the blood
and dust, and left in one of the rooms whilst we
prepared to receive our visitors. They did not arrive
quite punctually, and we went a little way to meet them,
and brought them back with us. As usual, tea was

OUR LANDLORD AND LANDLADY AT SEMENDRIA BRINGING OUR BREAKFAST.

To face p. 48.]

served in the garden, and our lesson begun there as well; but during the course of the latter the sky became darkened with storm clouds, and ere long a flash of lightning, followed by a terrific peal of thunder and a shower of hail, drove us indoors. We repaired to a room adjoining that in which we had left our snake. The storm was so fierce whilst it lasted, the lightning so vivid, the crashes of thunder so deafening, and the downpour of hail and rain so heavy, that for a few minutes all remained silent. Gradually, however, as the storm abated, we resumed our conversation, and were very soon busy at our lessons. For some reason or other I was rather more backward than usual on this occasion, and my teacher was on the point of administering a lecture to me, when a loud hiss, followed by a scream from Mademoiselle Ristovitch, startled us all. There, in the twilight, for it was now getting dark, we discerned our captive gliding across the floor. For one second Hiems and I stared at one another in blank dismay; all was commotion and panic. The three ladies, tucking up their dresses after the manner of the sex when crossing a muddy road, perched themselves on chairs. M. Ristovitch armed himself with the hearth brush, Hiems seized a stick, and I a wooden stool, and we advanced to attack the reptile, which retreated into a corner, and with erect head and fierce hisses stood at bay. The contest was short and sharp. The snake made a sudden dart at me, which, luckily, I succeeded in receiving on my stool, and the next minute my friends had struck it down, and I had

crushed its head. This affair made Madame Ristovitch so nervous and uncomfortable that her husband
decided on returning home at once. The storm had now
completely passed away. The western sky was still
bright and flushed with gold and crimson by the setting
sun, the moon had risen, and the stars were beginning
to twinkle. Altogether it was a beautiful evening. M.
Ristovitch took the lead on their homeward journey with
his wife, Hiems followed with Mademoiselle Ristovitch,
and I brought up the rear with Mademoiselle Miloikovitch.

Now whether it was due to the storm or to the fine
weather which followed, or to the influence of the planet
Venus, which certainly was twinkling very brightly just
then, or to the pale moonbeams, or to the lively
manner in which Mademoiselle Miloikovitch had
mounted a chair and maintained herself there during
our combat with the snake, I cannot say, but I felt
at that moment desperately in love with her.

For several minutes we walked on in silence, but
although I did not actually speak, I was several times
on the verge of doing so. What I wanted to ask her
was, "What is the Servian name for love?"

At last I did venture to speak, but the sound of my
voice frightened me. I could get no further than
"what." Three desperate efforts I made to get out the
phrase, but each time my voice and courage failed me.

Fortune, however, favours the brave, and at last she
had compassion, and helped me. The part of the road

we were now traversing was rather rough, and in the silvery moonlight I saw that Mademoiselle Ristovitch had taken Hiems' arm. I therefore ventured to offer my arm to my partner, and, to my great joy, she at once took it. What a thrill of delight I experienced when I felt her fingers resting on it! The contact, light as it was, inspired me with fresh courage, and clearing my throat I dashed at the sentence once more, and this time succeeded in getting it all out.

"If you please, mademoiselle, what is the Servian word for love?"

Mademoiselle Miloikovitch fixed her large dark eyes on me for a moment with an expression in which surprise and amusement were equally blended, and then, to my great disappointment and discomfiture, replied, "I have given one lesson to-day already, M. Alfred, and I certainly am not going to give you another now. Besides, there are lots of things I want to talk about. For instance, I want to know if you have ever been a soldier?"

"I have been a volunteer," replied I, proudly.

"Can you shoot well?" said she, looking at me approvingly.

"Not well for an English rifleman, who are the best shots in the world, still I could hit a man at two hundred yards," I replied.

"I wish I were a man instead of a woman," said she, with sudden energy, "I would enlist in our army immediately."

"What a singular wish," said I, considerably surprised.

"A singular wish, M. Alfred! Do you not know that my relatives have been murdered and my dear country overrun and rendered desolate by those hateful wretches—the Turks? What would you think if your own land were invaded by hordes of cruel barbarians, smiling villages and happy homes turned into blackened heaps of ruins, and innocent, defenceless men, women, and children shot down and hacked to pieces? It has been my cruel lot to see all this take place before my very eyes, and I care not what any one thinks, and I repeat it,—I long for vengeance, and I often think of going—woman as I am—to the front and firing a shot at our accursed enemies."

Mademoiselle Miloikovitch spoke with such fierce emphasis and excitement, that for a moment I was thunderstruck. At last I said, "Mademoiselle, I sympathise most deeply with you, and I am very certain that were I in your place, I should feel precisely as you do now."

"What," said she, eagerly, "would you recommend me to go to the front?"

"Heaven forbid, mademoiselle!" said I, "unless you went as a nurse; and even then I don't think it would be a wise step on your part, as you have had no training."

"What aggravating things you men are! You are all alike; you all say the same thing; and there's not a bit

of sense in a single word you utter! " said she petulantly; then with a laugh she added, " I expect you
think me very strange. All the same, soldiering apart,
I wish I were a man ! Your greedy sex monopolised all
the sensible occupations, and left us poor women nothing
but nursing and needlework."

"Pardon me, mademoiselle, but I do not think you
quite do justice to our unfortunate sex. In my humble
opinion, the ladies —who in the long run always have
their own way—have allotted all the really disagreeable
work to us men. Who works harder and gets worse
paid than the doctor? Who gets more abuse than the
lawyer, or more sneered at than the parson, or more hard
blows than the soldier, or is more hated than the
politician ? On the other hand, what can be more
delightful than looking after a number of merry,
innocent children, or more profitable than needlework,
which provides you with new dresses, etc. ? "

"M. Wright," said Mademoiselle Miloikovitch
sternly, at the same time withdrawing her hand from my
arm, "you are talking nonsense, and you know it. I
shall not walk with you if you continue to do so ! "

"My dear mademoiselle," said I, in considerable
alarm, "pray forgive me ; I most humbly apologise. Ah,
mademoiselle ! can you think I would presume intention-
ally to offend you ? " and I contritely tendered her my
arm again.

"I cannot say whether I will forgive you or not,"
replied the young lady, still walking apart from me,

"that will depend entirely upon your behaviour for the rest of the evening. Now I want you to tell me, if you can, why the professions should not be as open to women as they are to men?"

"At the present time, mademoiselle," replied I, "there is, in my humble opinion, no good objection, speaking theoretically, to women, who are fitted by taste and inclination, and have been suitably educated, entering the professions. Practically, I scarcely think the world sufficiently advanced for such a step. Women are, speaking generally, purer and more refined than men, and they exercise an immense influence over our sex for good, which may be termed a home influence. Take women away from home, and send them into the world as it now stands, what would happen? They might gain in intellect, but I believe they would suffer morally by the change, and their influence for good be converted into an influence for evil. With the spread, however, of real thoughtful religion and knowledge, and the mental elevation that will accompany them, men and women will be able to work indiscriminately together, and then their so doing will have a good effect rather than otherwise."

"And how long, oh! most profound philosopher," said Mademoiselle Miloikovitch, "do you think it will be before this will happen?"

"I cannot say," replied I. "I don't believe the world is ripe for it just yet. It rests very much with you ladies when it will take place. You have an instrument at your

disposal more powerful for moving the world than Archi-
medes' lever."

" What is that, M. le Philosophe ? " said she.

" The force of your example, mademoiselle. When
the ladies make up their minds to do a thing, it is said
they always do it. Now there are 500,000,000 ladies,
young and old, in the world. Let these 500,000,000
irresistible beings resolve that the world shall take a
decided step in the direction of goodness, progress, and
enlightenment ; and let them, with that end in view, one
and all, give us poor men the benefit of their powerful
example, and heigh-presto ! the change would be effected
at once."

" Do you mean to insinuate then, sir," said Mademoiselle Miloikovitch, with an air of mock gravity, " that
we ladies are not setting you a good example now ? "

" Far be it from me, mademoiselle, to insinuate anything so utterly false," replied I ; " but I thought it might
be possible for your sex, as a whole, to undertake the
measure more vigorously."

" Hum, M. Alfred, you are a provoking prevaricator.
I will wait for six months to see if the world profits by
my good example, and takes a step in the right direction ;
but if it shows no signs of improvement then, I will
become a professional woman at once. But here we are
at home, will you come in? No? Then adieu ! and
many thanks for your instructive and philosophical dis-
course."

" Adieu, mademoiselle," replied I, attempting to give

her hand a tender little squeeze ; " will you tell me next time the Servian for that little word ? "

" You must wait until next time, M. le Philosophe," said she, withdrawing her hand, " and see. Adieu again."

CHAPTER VII.

CLOSE to the old fort was a secluded spot by the river side. Here, morning and evening, Hiems and I were wont to bathe. The Servians tried to dissuade us, declaring that the river abounded in poisonous water-snakes. The weather was so intensely hot, and we were so fond of the water, that in spite of the alarm occasioned by this information, we bathed regularly, at least once a day. Neither of us ever saw a water-snake nor anything like one, but it is not impossible that some of the adders, of which there are great numbers close to the water's edge, may, for divers reasons known only to themselves, occasionally indulge in a swim in the river, and that this was the origin of the Semendrian belief in water-snakes.

The night after my stroll with Mademoiselle Miloiko-vitch, I was singularly sleepless. I lay thinking a long time of our conversation. I felt vexed at having been so timorous, and kept conjuring up in my mind's eye some bolder suitor stepping in before me and winning her affections. "Surely," I thought, "so beautiful and interesting a young lady must have shoals of admirers;" and tossing about on my bed, I resolved that next time

4

I would make a formal proposal, and secure her for myself at once. This notable resolution calmed me a little, and I presently dozed off, but my sleep was fitful and broken by all kinds of senseless dreams. At five o'clock I rose, determined to refresh myself for my day's work by a swim in the river. I tried hard to persuade Hiems to accompany me, but the only response elicited from him by my eloquent appeal was an inarticulate mumbling, followed by a loud snore, so I set off by myself.

Arrived at the bathing place I quickly undressed and plunged into the river, which here was very deep, and about one-fourth of a mile in width. I was a very indifferent swimmer, but the water was so pleasant that I struck out boldly, and was soon far out in the stream. The strong current carried me along for some distance, so that when I turned to swim back, I discovered, to my consternation, that I was a long way from the place where I had left my clothes, and was drifting towards a small row of huts which lies a little beyond the old fort. I did not wish to land in front of these huts, as people were already moving about on the shore, and I foolishly endeavoured to swim against the stream to the point from which I had started. By exerting myself violently I succeeded in making a little progress at first, but I was quite two hundred yards from the shore, and beginning to feel dreadfully tired. Still I struggled on, and succeeded in diminishing this distance by another fifty yards. By this time, however,

I was nearly exhausted. A kind of numbness began to creep over my limbs, and I could scarcely strike out at all.

Recognising my danger, I endeavoured to make straight for the shore, but the numbness continued to increase, and I soon saw that unless someone came to my assistance, I would be quite unable to get to land at all. Cursing the folly which induced me to venture out so far alone, I shouted again and again for help. No one seemed to hear me, and I despairingly renewed my struggles. I thought of Mademoiselle Miloikovitch and of Hiems, of dear old England, and the friends and relatives whom I might never see again. Then drowsiness came over me—with the dim, vague idea of how comfortable the cottages on the shore looked, and how bright and green were the trees behind them, then I lost all consciousness. Luckily for me, a fisherman on the other side of the river had seen me turn in the water, and noticing the little progress I made, started to my assistance just as my strength was beginning to fail me. I had a very narrow escape, for he saw me sink twice before he could reach me, and just caught me by the hair as I was going down for the third time. It was a long time before I recovered my consciousness. My first sensations were those of extreme misery and discomfort. There was a choking sensation at my throat, and I felt most horribly sick and faint. Then I was made to swallow some strong spirits, and on opening my eyes I saw, as it were, in a mist, Ibaum, Stephanovitch, Cutemoff, and my dear friend Hiems, the latter—

God bless him !—sobbing as if his heart would break, and
swearing at himself for not having gone with me to
bathe, and praying for my recovery, in one and the
same breath.   Dr. lbaum seemed scarcely less agitated,
and when I opened my eyes, he flung away the glass of
cordial he held in his hand, and rushed into my friend's
arms, and the two hugged and jerked each other about—
I can't say danced—in such a comical manner, that, ill
as I was, I could not help laughing.

"Hurrah ! hurrah ! hurrah !" shouted Hiems ; "he's
coming round fast ! Look there ; he's laughing ; hip, hip,
hurrah ! "

"Yes, yes ; he have smile wit his mouth.   I have seen
so mine self, eep ! eep ! oorah !" and the two danced
round again.   Meanwhile Stephanovitch and Cutemoff
had been working indefatigably (and, indeed, so had the
others, until I opened my eyes and their feelings over-
came them), trying different methods of artificial respira-
tion upon me, chafing my limbs, and putting hot
applications to my chest, etc. ; and at last they had
succeeded in completely restoring my temporarily
suspended animation.

"By Jove, doctor !" said Hiems, extricating himself
from Ibaum's embrace, "he's coming round grandly.
Let us make his bed comfortable for him, and he will
have a good sleep."

By this time I was able to breathe very well, and with
a heart overflowing with gratitude I tried hard to thank
my kind friends for their goodness, but they refused to

let me speak, and tucking me up in dry and warm
blankets, bade me go to sleep. As I felt very heavy
and sleepy and weary, I was not long in following their
advice. My last recollection of that memorable morning was seeing my dear old Hiems seated by my
bedside, looking anxiously into my face, and good Dr.
Ibaum stealing noiselessly about the room, now darken-
ing the windows, and now chasing a noisy little mosquito
from my bed.

But my troubles were not over yet.

On waking from my sleep I had a violent shivering fit,
followed by a sharp pain in my side, great difficulty in
breathing, and high fever. The water I had drawn into
my lungs caused a severe attack of pneumonia. For
some days I was in furious delirium, and whilst in this
condition the wildest and most extravagant fancies filled
my brain. Now I thought I was on the battle-field, surrounded by Bashi-Bazouks, who, in spite of my furious
resistance, bore me to the ground, and thrust their weapons
into my chest and side. Then again I would fancy I was
walking about in a beautiful meadow with Mademoiselle
Miloikovitch, plucking gorgeous flowers and offering them
to her. Suddenly a hollow moaning sound filled my ears,
and a vague and indefinable feeling of dread came over
me. Then, instead of Mademoiselle Miloikovitch, appeared
a terrible and menacing figure, and the hollow moaning
sound changed to a loud roar of advancing water, from
which I would try to escape ; but the figure by my side
held me fast, and the waters overtook and overwhelmed

me. This form of delirium was followed by a complete
unconsciousness, during which time I believe I must
have been asleep, for I awoke one morning to find the
pain in my chest and difficulty of breathing nearly gone,
and feeling comparatively comfortable. Hiems and Dr.
Cutemoff were in the room, standing near the window,
and talking in whispers. I had a vague idea that something had happened, but I could not recollect what,
so I called out in a voice so weak and strange that it
surprised me—

"Hulloh! Hiems, where am I, and what is the
matter?"

In a moment the two were at my bedside. "Thank
God, my dear boy," said Hiems fervently, "for your
recovery. You have been desperately ill. Once or twice
we actually gave you up. At one time you were fighting,
raging, and raving like a demon, so that it took three or
four of us to hold you down, and you called me an infernal Bashi-Bazouk, Dr. Cutemoff a vile Circassian, and
told Ibaum and Stephanovitch they were a couple of
Turkish devils, and that if we would let you get up and
try your hanging guard, you would take us all single-
handed. You told us fifty times over you were a British
subject, and dared us to touch you, on pain of incurring
the wrath of the British empire."

"What a trouble and nuisance I must have been to
you all!" said I, pressing Hiems' hand. "I am sure I
can never, never repay you for all your kindness."

"Shut up, old chap," said Hiems; "you've nothing

whatever to thank me for. The little I have been able to do I would have done for anybody who was as ill as you have been, much more then for an old friend. I'm sure, under similar circumstances, you would do the same for me."

"That I would, a thousand times over," replied I, gratefully.

"Very well then, you see we are quits. But now hold your tongue, old boy; you have done quite enough talking for the present. Hulloh! where's Cutemoff? Ah! here he comes with some beef-tea and jelly. What a regular trump he is, isn't he? Don't answer. So are they all."

And indeed nothing could have exceeded the kindness I received from all quarters, and I owe the kind friends who attended me during my illness a debt of gratitude I can never repay.

CHAPTER VIII.

THANKS to a sound constitution, I was soon up and about again, so that three weeks afterwards I was able to set to work at the hospital, and this, moreover, in spite of a severe disappointment which befell me in the temporary annihilation of any amatory designs upon Mademoiselle Miloikovitch. M. Ristovitch received a summons from the Skuptchine, or Servian Parliament, to proceed at once on business of importance to Paratchin, a town some sixty miles from Semendria, and not very far from Deligrad, which was at that time the headquarters of General Tchernaieff's army. As Mademoiselle Miloikovitch had relatives there, he decided upon taking her with him. Consequently, when I recovered, I found that my fair lady had gone, and that for the present I could hope for no opportunity of informing her of the state of my feelings.

A personage made his appearance at Semendria a day or two after I resumed work, who drove all thoughts of love-making out of my head. This was Baron von Tummy, the celebrated Austrian surgeon, who was acting at the time as Inspector-General of all the Servian hospitals. His advent was preceded by the arrival of a

large batch of wounded and invalided soldiers from the
front. They were so numerous that every available
corner in both hospitals was occupied. Most of the
invalids were suffering from dysentery, and were as ill
as they could be, and many of them emaciated to
skeletons. Many of the wounded soldiers, too, were
dangerously hurt, so that, as might be imagined, we all
had our hands pretty full. Baron Von Tummy was a
very remarkable man, both for intellect and personal
appearance. He was very short, very stout, and very
clever ; in fact, weighty both in mind and body. In
height he was perhaps five feet two inches, but he must
have been nearly two yards in circumference. He
might have been fifty years of age, and he had iron-gray
hair, beard, moustache, and whiskers, and a stern and
resolute expression. The day he arrived all the doctors
mustered at the hospital to receive him. Everything
was as neat and shipshape as possible, but though the
wards were clean, two things were painfully evident—the
defective ventilation and the overcrowding. Our first
impression of Baron Von Tummy was decidedly agreeable. Considering his great size he was remarkably
active, and waddled along at an astonishing rate. He
was dressed in the uniform of a colonel in the Servian
army—viz., a brown tunic with red facings, a row of gilt
buttons down the centre, and three gold stars on either
side of the collar, blue pantaloons, with a very broad red
stripe down the sides, and a naval officer's peaked cap.
He carried no sabre, but bore in his right hand a huge

white cotton umbrella, lined with blue, with which he shaded himself from the sun. The first thing the Baron did on entering the hospital was to shut up his umbrella, pull a very wry face, stop his nose with his fingers, and charge at the windows with the point of his gingham. Smash, crash, and crinnel! and a shower of glass descended on to the floor. Then, turning to me with startling abruptness, he said, in excellent English,—

" Phew, that's a d——d sight better, Mr. Englishman, isn't it ? "

" A great improvement, sir," said I.

The Baron's grimace and whimsical energy excited the risibility of the servants and soldiers present, and they all began to chuckle and grin. Von Tummy stopped short and glared around him with a fierce growl, and the alarmed bystanders checked their hilarity directly, all except one unhappy man, who did his best to restrain his mirth, but ineffectually, and broke every now and then into a smothered guffaw.

In an instant the redoubtable umbrella descended on his head with a sounding thwack, and as the man turned to flee, his departure was expedited by the forcible application of the Baron's foot to his back.

As soon as order was restored again, the Baron completed his inspection of the wards, formally presented Dr. Stephanovitch with a copy of a book he had published on hospital management, shook hands very affably with Hiems and myself, and took his leave.

On my expressing surprise to one of the doctors at the

baron's familiarity with the English language, he told me that he (the baron) could converse fluently in twelve European languages, and that curiously enough he paid especial attention to oaths and expletives, so that when annoyed he would sometimes swear in half a score of different tongues.

Some days after I received a despatch signed "Ludwig Von Tummy." It informed me that I was selected to take charge of a batch of forty wounded men who were to be sent from Semendria to Belgrade ; that I should have two Servian medical students as assistants, and that I must be in readiness to start by steamboat the next morning. Poor Hiems looked round to see if there was a despatch for him, and was sorely disappointed not to find one. However, he consoled himself with the reflection, that, had he been sent, he would have been deprived of the society of the charming Mademoiselle Ristovitch. Presently Ibaum and Stephanovitch looked in. They also had received orders from Von Tummy to get the wounded men in readiness. They congratulated me heartily on my good fortune in being selected for the service, but there was, at the same time, something mysterious in their manner. They nodded and winked and whispered to one another in a way that puzzled both Hiems and myself. It was evident that both wished to say something to me, but that neither liked to begin. At length Stephanovitch asked me in German whether I preferred the charge of sick men or wounded. I replied that it was immaterial to me, but that other

things being equal, sick men required less looking after.
" Ha," said little Ibaum, with an air of great satisfaction, " you will like bester to take ill people ? "

" No, I don't say that," I replied. " I merely say
that sick men will probably require less looking after."

" So—so—good—most good," said Ibaum, nodding
his head. Then they smiled and winked at one another,
and shook hands with me over and over again, and
departed, leaving the mystery unsolved.

The next morning we were up at six o'clock, and at
the hospital by half-past. There all was noise and
masterly inactivity. Several of the soldier servants were
lounging about, chattering away at the top of their voices.
A few were engaged in the removal of the wounded, but
were doing it in the most casual manner—joining in
the general conversation and exchanging repartees with
the loungers with the most perfect indifference to the
groans of their unhappy burdens. These unfortunate
creatures were deposited by twos in little carts littered
with straw and hay, and driven slowly to the landing-
place, there to await embarkation. Early as it was, Drs.
Ibaum and Stephanovitch were already there, superintending operations. As soon as the former saw me he came
forward, and greeting me cordially pressed me to have
some breakfast with him in the hospital. Believing
there was a lot of work to be done, I declined.

" My so good friend," said Ibaum, "there is not more
wounded men to go. They have all early this morning
gone ; there is the laster two ! "

"Goodness me!" said I; "you must have been up very early this morning."

"My dear friend," replied he, "I was very early to rise this morning. The Baron Von Tummy is a very punctual man,—oh, most punctuallest! So come in, you, and the dear Hiems, and have a few breakfast here!" It was quite true,—all the invalids who were to be removed had gone, so we yielded to Dr. Ibaum's hospitable importunity, and had a "few breakfast" with him. During the progress of the meal I noticed our host once or twice exchanging signals with Stephanovitch, and wondered thereat, but reflecting that their idiosyncracies were no concern of mine, I went on with my breakfast, and said nothing.

As soon as the meal was concluded, we went to the river side, where the wounded men were awaiting the arrival of the steamboat, which was to convey them away. The latter was now within half a mile of us, and rapidly approaching. As soon as Ibaum saw the boat, he produced a field-glass, and adjusting its focus somewhat pompously, scanned the steamer with a haughty and commanding air. Suddenly he turned very white, dropped the glass out of his hands, and uttering a hollow groan, literally staggered against Stephanovitch. The countenance of the latter, too, underwent a sudden and ghastly change, like that of a man who is seized with an attack of cramp in the stomach, and both of them uttered simultaneously the name Von Tummy! Following the direction of their glances, I saw on board the vessel,

and looking over its side, the fierce, resolute countenance of the illustrious Von Tummy! But though the
great man's expression was ferocious, yet, as he was not
looking at either of the terror-stricken Servian doctors,
I was quite at a loss to account for their panic. Meanwhile the steamer glided up to the landing-place, and
the object of their dread waddled ashore, and, strange to
say, saluted us all with gracious cordiality, and then
gave orders that a stack of hay, which stood in a field
close by, should be demolished, and the hay spread over
the deck for the wounded men to lie on. Now it so
happened that the hay belonged to a farmer who intended consigning it to Belgrade for sale to the military
authorities, and who hoped to reap a large profit by the
transaction.

The consternation of this individual, who happened
to be standing by when the hospital servants began to
carry out the baron's injunctions, was piteous. With
anguish depicted on every feature, he hastened to Von
Tummy's side and energetically remonstrated against
this summary proceeding. The baron's reply was a
terrific scowl and a savage ejaculation, which evidently
meant "Shut up!" The foolhardy farmer, however, persisted in pleading for his goods. The baron gave him
another black look, and then, as lightning flashes fall
from a storm-cloud, leaped upon him, and inflicted, first
a heavy blow upon his nose, then a second on his
stomach, which doubled him up, and finally put him
to flight by a volley of kicks. Meanwhile the soldiers,

with the usual Servian indolence, were very slowly pulling down the stack and trailing small bundles of hay towards the ship. The lazy spectacle exasperated the irascible and energetic Von Tummy beyond measure. Seizing a long carter's whip from a bystander, he rushed amongst them and lashed into them furiously, shouting with every stroke " Heite ! " (make haste !), followed by a string of untranslatable and unsavoury Servian and German oaths. The effect of this well-timed onslaught was excellent. The demolition of the haystack was greatly accelerated, and the hay was promptly conveyed on board and arranged on the deck. Hiems, with his hateful love of punning, remarked, with a grin, " That it was but natural that a whipping should make the Servians smart," a joke which, in spite of my respect for the baron, nearly made me ill.

Apparently satisfied and restored to good humour by the results of his severity, the baron linked his arm in mine, and leaning on me, said that he would now inspect the wounded men.

As we approached the convoy of invalids Ibaum and Stephanovitch were once more seized with the same unaccountable panic—especially Ibaum, who hurriedly muttering something about an operation which must be immediately performed, fairly turned tail and bolted. Stephanovitch, though pale as death, stood his ground.

Arrived beside one of the patients, Von Tummy, apparently not noticing the singular conduct of the two

Servian doctors, asked the man what was the matter
with him.

"Dysentery, sir."

"What!" roared the baron, "aren't you wounded,
then?"

"Oh, wretched fool!" interposed Stephanovitch,
"what are you talking about? Your Excellency,"
turning to Von Tummy, "the man has a severe wound
in the head, and does not know what he is saying."

"I see no wound in his head, sir," replied the baron,
giving Stephanovitch a keen glance. "Why ——"
(here Von Tummy thundered forth a string of expletives
in half-a-dozen different languages), "the man isn't
wounded at all! Get out of that" (tearing off the
sick man's coverlet); "be off!" (giving him a kick, and
then to next soldier), "What's the matter with you?"
"Dysentery." "Oh, indeed ——" (oaths), "take
that, and that!" and with a kick and a thump he sent
him about his business as well, and so on, right through
the convoy, until he had weeded out all the sick, leaving
only the wounded there. The spectacle, in spite of its
cruelty, was ludicrous enough. There was the corpulent
Von Tummy, rushing furiously hither and thither amongst
the half-clad, emaciated Servians, whilst they stalked
away in all directions, holding their garments about
them, as fast as their wasted legs would carry them.

It seems that both Ibaum and Stephanovitch greatly
preferred surgery to medicine, and when they received
instructions to send away forty of their wounded, con-

ceived the idea of getting rid of several of their sick at
the same time. They were under the impression that
Von Tummy was on his way to the front, where he
would probably stay some time, and hence their terror
when they recognised him on board the steamboat.
Stephanovitch received a terrible lecture from the
baron, but as for Dr. Ibaum, I believe he got off scot-
free. Nothing happened after this to hinder the embarkation of the remaining wounded, and with a kindly
word of advice from Von Tummy I went on board,
and we started.

The voyage was quite uneventful and very pleasant.
The wounded enjoyed the fresh air immensely after
their long confinement in the close wards of the hospital.
Thanks to Von Tummy's influence, a large awning was
spread over the deck, which shielded them from the
rays of the sun. They had grapes from the Prince's
vineyard, and tobacco, supplied by the Russian com-
mittee, and were fairly comfortable on the whole. The
boat stopped at Topchidere, a place about a mile beyond
Belgrade. A large concourse of people were awaiting
our arrival, for it happened that my convoy was the first
that had been sent by water, consequently a good deal
of fuss was made about it.

Amongst the lookers-on I noticed a slovenly little
personage in a dingy white holland tunic. He wore
spectacles and a shabby beard and moustache, and
seemed to me to be very seedy and poverty stricken.
Thinking that he was probably looking out for a job,

5

I motioned to him to lend a hand to the men who were carrying out the wounded soldiers, and tendered him a franc.

Never shall I forget the look of disgust and offended pride with which he declined my well-meant offer.

" Sir," said he to me in French, " do you know who I am?"

I shook my head.

" I am Dr. Yermaylaff Giggleivitch, Chevalier of the Order of St. Michael and St. George, and chief surgeon to His Imperial Majesty the Czar of all the Russias." So saying, he gave me another withering glance, and turned away.

When I had delivered my charges into the hands of those appointed to receive them, I proceeded, under the guidance of my two assistants, to an hotel,—yclept the Hotel London,—remarkable, as I learnt to my discomfort, for the extraordinary number of unsavoury insects which infested its bedrooms. Von Tummy's instructions to me were to return by the boat, which would leave Belgrade at seven the following morning. So after strolling about and amusing myself in various ways for the rest of the day, I turned in about nine o'clock in the evening. My two assistants had left me early in the day, and gone to visit their sweethearts, under promise to return early and to be up in time for the boat, and I had arranged with the landlord to call us all at five the next morning. I was somewhat tired when I went to bed, and threw myself on the mattress with that satisfaction which one feels after a long and fatiguing day. But I was doomed to get no sleep that night. Just as I was dozing off, a burning bite on the face aroused me, followed by another on the hand, and another on the foot. Springing up and striking a light, I discovered that I was assailed by legions of insects that crawled and insects that hopped; in fact, in imminent danger of being devoured alive. They came marching down the walls in battalions, and they dropped on to me from the ceiling. I spent the whole night in doing battle with my adversaries—destroying them by scores on the wall, on the coverlet, and on the floor; nor did the carnage cease until four o'clock in the morning. Then I began to dress, and whilst sitting down for a moment, had the misfortune to fall fast asleep.

Now had the landlord done his duty and called me, as he promised, at five, all would have been well. As it was, I slept on until eight o'clock, and of course lost the boat. My two assistants, who might have called me, and did not do so, alleged in excuse that their respect for me prevented them from disturbing my repose. In reality, the scamps wanted another day's holiday at Belgrade. There was nothing for it but to wait until the next day, as any other kind of conveyance to Semendria was unprocurable. From what I had seen of Von Tummy's disposition, I expected that this unfortunate mischance would get me into a scrape, and so it proved; but I anticipate.

Whilst I was at breakfast, a party of twelve or fourteen

Russian officers came into the coffee-room, making a prodigious clanking with their sabres, and occupied most of the vacant tables. I looked at them with considerable interest. They were of all ages and sizes,—from six feet two inches to five feet nothing,—and apparently of every rank, from the polished noble to the unlettered boor. One group, in particular, attracted my attention. It consisted of three persons. The senior member of the party was a well-made man of medium height, with finely-cut features, blue eyes, and a heavy, blonde moustache, and completely bald. His air was commanding, and by the respect shown him by his companions, he was evidently a personage of some importance. Of his companions one was a very tall, fair-haired young man, with one of the handsomest faces I have ever seen, and the other was a slightly-made, pleasant-looking man of average height, and about twenty-eight years of age. They drank champagne freely, and seemed in a very jovial mood. Whilst gazing at the group, I became aware that some one was dodging about me in a very odd manner, and looking up, I saw a little Russian officer, with a face like a monkey, dancing backwards and forwards behind me. He had a heavy scimitar at his side and a revolver in his belt, and was pointing with an expression of intense contempt at the red cross on my coat sleeve. By-and-by I saw that this singular demonstration meant to indicate to me his opinion that men with the cross on their arms were cowards; for, after pointing to the cross with a grimace and a sniff, he pretended to run away in a great fright. Presently he advanced boldly up to me with a menacing air, and drew his revolver. Not understanding his object, and not liking his rudeness, I drew mine, and watched him closely, fully determined to use it if necessary.

What might have happened I do not know. Fortunately the bald-headed gentleman with the big moustache said something to him in a sharp, authoritative tone of voice, and he slunk away, when the tall, handsome young fellow came forward, and making me a polite bow, said in French,—

" Permit me, sir, to apologise in the name of the Russians here present for that fellow's rudeness ! "

I replied that no apology was necessary ; whereupon he made me another polite bow, and we shook hands cordially. The Russian courteously invited me to drink a glass of wine with him and his friends. I accepted the invitation, and as I approached their table, both the bald-headed officer and the slim young man with the agreeable countenance rose and treated me to a friendly shake of the hand. They informed me that they were officers of the Russian Imperial Guard, and were going as volunteers to the front, and would leave Belgrade next morning for Semendria, by boat, *en route* for Deligrad. I told them we should be fellow-passengers as far as Semendria, at which they seemed very pleased. After the wine we had coffee and cigarettes, and all became very sociable. Several of the other Russians joined in the conversation. I observed, however, that they always treated the bald-headed individual with great deference, and I noticed also, with some pride, that my gutta-percha boots attracted considerable attention and several approving smiles ; at least, they appeared to me to be so. Two of the Russians, however, took exception to them. One of them told me that my boots, though possibly good in theory, were not practical ; the other, a rough-looking fellow of gigantic stature, with a shock head of yellow hair and a shaggy moustache, offered me, through the medium of an interpreter (for he could speak no language but his own), another pair of boots, expressing at the same time the utmost disgust for my favourite gutta-perchas. I was a little bit hurt at his apparent inability to appreciate their merit, so I requested the interpreter (one of the Imperial Guard officers) politely to decline his kind offer for me. My refusal apparently offended this singular person very much, for he frowned fiercely, and said something in an angry tone.

"Sir," said the interpreter to me, "he is much disappointed at your declining his offer, and trusts you will reconsider the matter."

I replied that I thanked him very much, but having plenty of boots of my own, it was quite unnecessary for me to deprive him of a pair of his. At this the shock-headed gentleman waxed exceedingly wrath, and darting a fierce look at me, struck the table a blow with his clenched fist.

"Sir," said the Imperial Guardsman, "I think that

"I NOTICED ALSO, WITH SOME PRIDE, THAT MY GUTTA-PERCHA BOOTS ATTRACTED
CONSIDERABLE ATTENTION."

To face p. 78.]

perhaps it would be prudent of you to accept his offer, otherwise he may want to fight you."

"Bless my soul!" said I, laughing; "if he looks at it in that light, I'll accept his offer at once;" and walking up to him, I nodded my head at him, and extended my hand in token of friendship. Before taking my hand, this susceptible giant appealed to the guardsman, and then seizing my hand in his enormous paw, squeezed it almost into a jelly, pushed me into a chair, and dashed out of the room. In a minute or two he returned with a pair of top boots under his arm, and kneeling down, whipped off my beloved india-rubbers, and put his own on my feet in their stead. Then sitting down and leaning his elbows on the table he supported his chin on his hands, and taking a good look at me, told me that I was very like a dear friend of his, who had been killed in battle, *à propos* of which he said he would like to ask me a question.

"Some time ago, I was engaged in a battle with the Turkomans. We were greatly outnumbered, and for five hours were exposed to a terrible fire. For the first four hours I felt calm and cool, as a soldier ought to feel under fire, but after that I became, all at once, terribly frightened. I want to know how it was that I should all at once lose my presence of mind.

Having delivered himself of this question, the burly dragoon officer—for such he proved to be—rested his chin on his hands again, and looked at me with a wistful earnestness of expression that indicated the anxiety with which he awaited my answer.

For the moment I was fairly puzzled. Then I asked him if he had a wife and children. He replied with ecstatic energy, "Yes, yes, yes!" and kissing his hand fervently, placed it first about two feet from the ground, then he kissed it again and placed it a foot higher, then again, raising it a foot higher still, which I understood to mean that he had a wife and three children of the sizes indicated.

"Well then, sir," said I, "I think your conduct on that battle field can be easily explained. During the first four hours you thought only of your duty, and consequently feared nothing, but in the fifth hour you remembered your wife and children, and that thought unnerved you!"

No sooner had my reply been explained to the dragoon, than he sprang up with much energy, upsetting his chair and nearly capsizing the table, and then folding me in his arms, smothered my face with kisses, exclaiming that I had taken a great load off his mind, for he had fretted about his conduct on that occasion ever since. Then, summoning the waiter, he ordered a bottle of champagne, and filled a glass tankard up to the brim for me, and one for himself, and clashing his glass against mine, tossed off his wine at a single draught. I had already had one tumblerful of champagne, and consequently could drink very little of the wine, which greatly astonished and disappointed him, but he was pacified when I explained that I scarcely ever took wine at home.

"Why," said he, in a tone of surprise, "in Russia I drink a bottle of brandy and five bottles of wine every day."

In the afternoon, the young officer who had remarked that my boots were unpractical, and whose name was Mouravioff, proposed that we should go for a walk, and a party, consisting of five or six of the Russians and myself, went in the direction of the arsenal. On our way we happened to pass the palace. Princess Natalie was at the time lying ill there, and an edict had been issued forbidding people either to drive or ride past. The princess was exceedingly popular, and the good people of Belgrade, in their anxiety for her recovery, carried out the edict to the letter, and when passing the palace used to speak in whispers and walk on tip-toe. I was not aware of this at first, and consequently was somewhat surprised and amused to see scores of people— soldiers, civilians, and women—whispering together and walking about as lightly as possible, like nurses in a sick-room, but when I knew the cause, this popular demonstration of sympathy touched me considerably, and heightened my respect for the Servian character. Suddenly the silence was broken by the clattering of a horse's hoofs and the yelping of a cur! Who should appear upon the scene, mounted upon a large chestnut horse, but Colonel Bragg! He sat his horse pretty well, but from his fiery complexion, and the way he swore at the dog, which bayed furiously at his horse's heels, I fancy he must have been intoxicated. That, at least, is a charitable supposition!

The cur yelped and snapped at the horse, making it rear and plunge in a way that threatened to unseat the gallant colonel, who, livid with rage, cursed until he was hoarse.

For fully five minutes a frightful war of sounds continued—the dog growling and barking, the colonel roaring and swearing, and the horse kicking and striking sparks from the rough pavement with his hoofs. Suddenly the terrible Bragg changed his tactics, and drawing his sabre made a vigorous down cut at the dog. The blow was well aimed; the dog's head rolled on the stones. Then sheathing his weapon, the colonel trotted along, twirling his moustache with an air of triumphant ferocity on his truculent face. Undeterred, however, by the awful fate of the cur, a presumptuous gendarme took upon himself the enforcement of the edict in the colonel's case, and fearlessly confronting him, forbade him to ride further in that direction.

"Get out of my way, you —— idiot! What's the matter with you?" said the colonel, contemptuously, putting on a tremendous expression, and endeavouring to spur his horse past the bold gendarme. The "bold gendarme," however, laid hold of the bridle.

"Will you take your hand off my bridle?" shouted the colonel.

The gendarme stood firm, whereupon, uttering one

To face p. 82.]   COLONEL BRAGG.

of his choicest oaths, the colonel struck him on the face, and making his horse rear at the same time, succeeded in shaking him off. Then invoking a lot of the most *bizarre* and *recherché* maledictions I ever heard on his discomfited adversary, the twice triumphant Bragg rode off.

" Do English officers usually behave like that ? " asked Mouravioff, sarcastically.

" Never," replied I, indignantly ; " they are gentlemen. As for this Colonel Bragg, I believe he is an American adventurer. I am quite certain he is not an English officer."

When we got out into the open country we threw ourselves on the grass beneath a shady tree, and refreshed ourselves with a nip from our flasks and a whiff of tobacco smoke.

" M. Wright," said the irrepressible Mouravioff, "what will England do when Russia declares war against her ? "

" She will probably fight," said I.

" How can she fight us ? She has only 100,000 men, we have 3,000,000. Moreover, her soldiers, though they are brave, cannot stand extremes of cold and heat like ours."

" Why, sir," replied I, " they did very well in the Crimea, where it was cold enough, and they contrive to get on in India, where it is rather warm."

" Still, sir, the fact remains that you have only 100,000 men."

"On the contrary, we have a great many more: 120,000 regulars, 150,000 militia, and 200,000 volunteers ; besides," said I, "there are all our sailors, numbering 180,000. These sailors," I continued, waxing warm in defence of our national prowess, "are all armed with pistols and cutlasses like this" (pointing to the one I wore) ; "and they have a peculiar kind of guard, called the hanging guard, which I will show you, which renders them invincible as swordsmen. This," said I, drawing my cutlass, and putting myself into my very best hanging-guard position, "is how British sailors fight!" and I looked round to see what effect my formidable attitude produced upon the Muscovites. They were all smiling, doubtless with admiration.

"If English soldiers fight like that," said Mouravioff, in an altered tone, "they must indeed be invincible!"

*   *   *   *   *

On our return to the Hotel London we separated for the night, under promise to meet again at five o'clock the next morning, and I retired to bed—but, alas! not to sleep, for fresh swarms of insects, as if to avenge their deceased comrades, kept me awake until three in the morning, when having slaughtered the greater part of my tormentors, I at last managed to snatch some repose.

CHAPTER IX.

BANG! bang! bang! Thump! thump! thump! Bang! thump! bang! thump! bang! These were the sounds which aroused me the next morning; the landlord and the Russians were hammering at the door.

"Hulloh, Mr. Englishman!" said one of the Russians, when at length I appeared, "you sleep pretty soundly."

"I daresay," said I, rubbing my eyes. "I am very tired; I have hardly slept a wink through insects."

"Bah, monsieur," said another, "you will not make a good campaigner if you cannot put up with a few fleas."

"I suppose one can get used to all things in time," replied I, a little bit nettled; "but at present I must say I am not quite used to the disgusting vermin one meets with in this place."

"Certainly, certainly," replied the Russian; "but meanwhile breakfast is ready, and the steamboat starts at seven o'clock."

I dressed in a trice, and went down into the coffee-room, where my assistants and the Russians were

assembled at the breakfast table. I sat down, and
soon had occasion to ask the Russian next me to pass
me the salt. To my surprise, however, he absolutely
refused, and I had to rise and get it for myself. The
young officer who had apologized to me on the preceding day for his countryman's rudeness explained,
that amongst Russians of a certain class a superstition
exists, that passing salt to comparative strangers leads to
a quarrel.

After breakfast the Russians called for champagne,
and concluded their last meal at Belgrade, before going
to the front, by toasting the Czar and singing their
national anthem. We then all proceeded to the river-
side, and embarked in good time. We were favoured
again with the most lovely weather. After a pleasant
voyage of a few hours the boat drew up at the Semendria
landing-place. I was so charmed with the companion-
ship and courtesy of the Russians that I invited them
to the rooms that Hiems and I held in common. Ten
of them, including the tall young officer who first spoke
to me, his bold friend Mouravioff, and the dragoon who
gave me the boots, accepted my invitation, and I was preparing to leave with them, when the terrible Von Tummy
planted his substantial corporation in front of me, and
fixing his piercing eyes upon me, said, with a dark frown,
" *Well, sir!*"

So sharply did he speak and so stern were his looks,
that for the moment I was dumbfoundered. The
Russians, however, were standing round looking on.

With a bland smile, therefore, I extended my right hand, and said in accents of hearty cordiality,—

" Ah, baron ! How d'ye do ? "

My impudence surprised the baron; for a moment he looked at me in speechless indignation. Then stamping one of his ponderous feet on the deck he asked me what the —— I meant by not returning yesterday.

" It was an accident, sir," replied I.   " I had the misfortune to lose the boat."

" It's a lie, sir ! You wanted to lose the boat ! " roared the angry baron. " Be off to your quarters, sir.   I'll talk to you by-and-by ! "

" I am not in the habit of telling lies," I replied, imprudently.

" How dare you answer me, you impudent English jackanapes ! " thundered Von Tummy, shaking his fist in my face.

" And how dare you call me jackanapes, you two-penny-halfpenny Austrian baron ! " screamed I, beside myself with passion.

Just then Hiems, who had heard this dialogue with much alarm, came to my rescue, and putting his hand over my mouth, attempted to drag me away, saying,—

" Don't be a fool, old fellow ; you're spoiling all your chances ! "

" I'll dismiss you from the service," roared Von Tummy.

" Dismiss me, and be hanged ! " shouted I, succeed-ing, after a desperate struggle, in tearing Hiems' hand from my mouth ; but this was all I could say, for the next moment my friend carried me bodily away. Once removed from the baron's irritating presence, I recovered my equanimity. The Russians were full of sympathy for me, and when I told them the baron had called me a jackanapes, which I explained to them meant a conceited, insignificant, monkey-like fellow, their friendly indignation knew no bounds.

"Resign your post as surgeon at this hospital, monsieur," said the bald-headed gentleman, "and come with us to the front."

"Yes, yes, come with us to the front!" cried the other Russians in chorus.

Matters had gone so far, that in spite of Hiems' remonstrances and disappointment, I decided to accept their invitation, and told them that I would be glad to cast in my lot with theirs, and accompany them as a volunteer. My decision was hailed with great applause. Even Hiems reluctantly admitted that after what had taken place it would be impossible for me to remain under Von Tummy; so I wrote the latter a letter, regretting my hasty conduct, and sending him, at the same time, my resignation as assistant surgeon at Semendria. To this I received no response.

We spent the rest of the afternoon in the most festive manner,—drinking success and rapid promotion to one another; and all separated for the night in the highest spirits, except poor Hiems, who took my approaching departure very much to heart, and would not be comforted, in spite of all my efforts to console him.

CHAPTER X.

THE next morning, as I was sitting at breakfast with Hiems, Mouravioff and another Russian came to the door and told me that the waggons that were to convey us to Deligrad were waiting at the Lion Hotel. I had already packed up my small stock of wearing apparel in my knapsack and a large travelling bag. The former I strapped on to my shoulders, the latter my good-natured landlord assisted me to carry. Hiems accompanied me to the hotel, and we walked there in silence, for now that the moment for parting had come we both felt heavy-hearted. I noticed that the bald-headed officer—instead of sharing a waggon with two or three others, like the rest of us—had a well-appointed carriage, and started a few minutes before us. Our waggons were of the very roughest description, more like large hencoops with the tops off, on wheels, than travelling conveyances. They boasted of neither springs nor seats, the place of the latter being supplied by bundles of rushes. Three of us were stowed in each of these vehicles, mine being the last of the train. A large crowd assembled by the hotel to witness our departure. Just before we started, Drs. Ibaum and

6

Stephanovitch appeared upon the scene, and wished me
" God speed " with much heartiness and fervour; then
Hiems gave me a last squeeze of the hand and " God
bless you," and we were off, amidst a waving of handkerchiefs and fezzes, and a shout of " Jivio " from the
crowd. My companions in the car were Mouravioff
and the handsome young officer who first spoke to me,
and whose name I learned was Savrimovitch. Both
were officers of the Russian Imperial Guard. We were
rather silent for the first half-hour or so. Probably we
were all of us thinking of home and home friends; at
least I know I was. But the broiling heat of the sun and
the terrific jolting of the car were fatal to sentimental
contemplation. Our coachman was a tall, narrow-
chested, round-shouldered individual, who sat in front
of us with his head on a level with his knees, and taking
no notice of anything or anybody, devoted all his
energies to humming a wearisomely monotonous ditty
in an utterly disagreeable falsetto. Our horse's appearance was strangely in keeping with that of his driver.
He was, without exception, the very scraggiest and most
dejected looking specimen that I ever saw, and his pace
was the slowest of slow jog trots.

The road along which we were driving was crossed
every few hundred yards by a drain about a foot deep
and eighteen inches wide, into which the trunk of a tree
had been rolled to enable vehicles to pass. The casual
Servian wayside authorities apparently made no effort to
select trees of the same size as the trenches ; some were

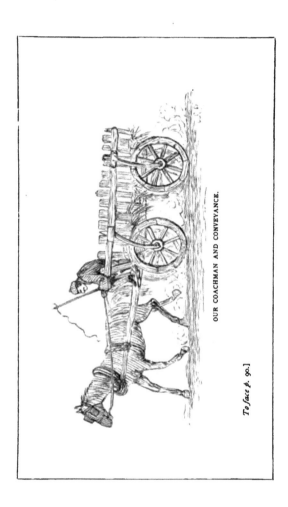

OUR COACHMAN AND CONVEYANCE.

To face p. 90.]

too big, and projected six inches above the level of the
roadway, others were too small.

Our coachman's method of getting over these trenches
was peculiar. When within twenty or thirty yards of one
of them, he would shout out something, which I suppose
meant "Hold on," urge his horse into a gallop, and
go straight at it. The result, as may be conceived, was
extremely shocking to the occupants.

Our first experience of one of these trenches may be
better imagined than described. The waggon struck the
obstacle with a crash, and bounded over it with a smash
and a bump, shooting me a foot or so into the air, and
bringing the back of my head into such violent contact
with the side of the car, that for the moment I was
stunned. My companions fared no better. When I
came to they were lying—one on the top of the other—at
the bottom of the car, and struggling to get up. The
only one of us who seemed not to have suffered was the
coachman. He was sitting just as before, humming
precisely the same ditty, and our Rosinante had relapsed
into the same jog-trot again. We requested this musical
Jehu to be more careful the next time he took us over
one of these trenches. He stopped his humming for a
moment, and without turning his head, replied that he
would, and then droned away again at his ditty as mono-
tonously as ever. His idea of being more careful,
however, was to go over the next trench with a little
extra spurt, so that we got as badly shaken as before.
This was too much for our equanimity, so as soon as we

had got over this second bruising, we held a brief council of war, which ended in our pulling coachee off his seat, and bundling him into a corner of the car with one or two gentle thumps, by way of reprisal for the knocking about he had inflicted on us. My two companions then desired me to drive, remarking that all Englishmen could ride and drive. Now it unfortunately happened that I could do neither, having been brought up in London with no opportunity of learning. However, I had seen people drive often enough to know something about the *modus operandi*, and being most desirous of maintaining the honour of my country, I, with many secret misgivings, but with much outward show of cheerfulness, took the reins. For some time, fortune favoured me. Savrimovitch and Mouravioff, thinking all was right, entered into a little *tête-à-tête* conversation, without troubling themselves about me. The next few trenches, too, were provided with trunks of about the right size, and the road was nearly straight. True, I failed to keep the cart in the middle of the road, still, by constantly working at the reins, I succeeded in keeping the horse out of the hedge on either side. At last we came to a sharp turn. By pulling strongly at the near side rein I got the horse round the corner in grand style, but unluckily forgot to loosen the rein, so the stupid old creature ran right into the hedge. The wheel ran up the bank, the waggon turned over, pitching us all into the road, and upsetting the horse as well. For a minute we all lay in the dust without attempting to move—I, because I was so much astonished at what had taken place, the Russians because they were a good deal shaken, and. because our crafty Servian coachman, with an eye to saving himself, had contrived to fall on the top of them. Then we were suddenly roused to action by our venerable steed, which, possessed with an unwonted spirit of friskiness, began to kick so vigorously that it threatened soon to make matchwood of the waggon. I was on my feet in a moment, and running to the horse's head forced it to the ground again and sat on it, after the manner of London cabmen in similar emergencies. Neither Mouravioff nor Savrimovitch were much hurt, and shaking off the coachman, who was reclining comfortably on the top of them, they came to my assistance. The coachman did not offer to help us, but sat down in the middle of the road, sobbing and wringing his hands in a most dismal and lackadaisical manner, and praying his "dear Gospodin" horse not to kick his cart quite into little bits. However, we managed to right the cart. and set the horse on its legs again, and I resigned the reins to Savrimovitch, who proved an excellent driver, and we soon found ourselves in Jagodina—a large straggling town of about 10,000 inhabitants. Here we joined the rest of our party. Jagodina has acquired some local celebrity from its manufacture of wooden flasks and water-bottles. Some of these are very quaint and pretty. I became the possessor of one, under rather singular circumstances.

We had started again, and were driving through the

outskirts of the town, when an old peasant came running after us in great distress, and asked if any of our party was a doctor. He was referred to me, and I ascertained that his grandchild was in a fit. On following him into a cottage hard by, I saw an old woman, holding on her lap a fine boy, about a year old, in strong convulsions. I lanced the child's gums, which were much swollen, and putting him into a warm bath, had the satisfaction of seeing him come round. Before I left, the old couple blessed me with touching fervour, and begged me so hard to accept a wooden bottle that they had made themselves, that I felt constrained to take it.

The road between Jagodina and Paratchin, the next large town that we stopped at, is very good. It runs through a beautiful and fertile tract of country, covered with vast groves of plum trees, apple orchards, and vineyards. The scenery, moreover, became more picturesque as we went on. The ground undulated considerably, whilst the horizon was bounded by a lofty range of blue mountains. Between us and them, and at a considerably lower level than the road, was a beautifully wooded and well-watered plain. As the evening advanced the weather became very close and sultry, and a severe thunderstorm broke upon us before we reached Paratchin.

It was about half-past ten and pitch dark when we arrived, and we were all wet and very uncomfortable. The two or three hotels in the place were full, for a body of cavalry and two battalions of infantry had entered the town earlier in the evening, and they seemed to have taken up all the available accommodation. To add to our misery, the rain began to fall again in torrents. As a last resource we went to the Commissary of Police, and requested him to find us quarters. That worthy, however, shook his head, and said he was afraid it was impossible, but he would do the best he could, and sent a gendarme to take us to all the likely places. The gendarme proved a humbug. He walked us about fruitlessly for half an hour, and then quietly gave us the slip, leaving us more wet and miserable than ever. Under these circumstances we began to make up our minds to pass the night as well as we could in our cart, and with that object we made tracks for the market-place, where we had left it in charge of our Servian coachman. But lo! when we got there, both cart and driver had vanished! We now became desperate, and going into the coffee-room of the nearest hotel, we ordered some supper, intending to remain in the room all night. The place was crowded with Servian officers and soldiers talking, eating, drinking, singing, smoking, gambling, and sleeping. The uproar was tremendous, and the atmosphere, composed of steam from their wet clothing and tobacco smoke, particularly dense. We succeeded, however, in getting a corner to ourselves and making a first-rate supper. Then we strolled outside, to smoke a cigarette before going to sleep. On the way out, I noticed a door which had been left ajar. Curiosity impelled me to push it wide open, and I beheld a large, well-lit room with—oh, rapturous spectacle!— twenty comfortable-looking beds ranged round it. None of them were tenanted. My mind was made up at once, and I resolved at all hazards to sleep in one of them. True, they were engaged, as was evident from caps, swords, cloaks, and revolver cases laid on them, but that was a minor consideration. Running after Mouravioff and Sarvimovitch, I led them back to this room. They also went into ecstacies and appropriated beds. I tore off my sopping wet and clinging garments in the twinkling of an eye, and clapped on some dry things out of my knapsack, and jumping into the bed I had selected, removed the late owner's sword, revolver, etc., tucked myself under the coverlet, and wishing my comrades good-night, was asleep in no time.

How long I had been asleep I don't know, but I was roused by some one giving me a thump and dragging me on to the floor. Looking up, I became aware that the hideous little Russian who had insulted me in Belgrade was standing over me, grinning with rage, and cursing me in his guttural language with fierce volubility. Infuriated at this treatment, which was not perhaps altogether unjustifiable under the circumstances, I sprang to my feet and hit the Muscovite a blow on the nose that sent him reeling to the opposite side of the room. In a second his sabre flashed out of its sheath, and I had just time to put my eyeglass in my eye and raise my cutlass, when he aimed a desperate cut at my head. In my hurry, I quite forgot the hanging guard, and put up my weapon anyhow, and such was the force of his blow that it nearly struck it out of my hand, and made my fingers tingle for some minutes afterwards. I could see from the way the fellow handled his sword that he knew more about fencing than I did, still the blow on his nose had made his eyes water, and interfered with his sword play so much, that he had to stop every now and then to wipe away the tears. By nimbly jumping about, and by the lucky interposition every now and then of my cutlass between myself and the enemy, I contrived to avoid his cuts and thrusts ; and, indeed, if my eyeglass would have stopped in my eye, I think I should soon have vanquished him, but each time I made up my mind to try to disarm him, the eyeglass fell out. Nevertheless, I managed to strike several vigorous blows at him, which I flatter myself he had some difficulty in parrying.

At length, by a lucky chance, I snatched up my knapsack with my left hand, hurled it with such skill and dexterity at my adversary, that it struck him full in the chest, momentarily deprived him of breath, and jerked his sword out of his grasp. Then, without giving him time to recover himself, I closed with him, and we rolled over on the floor together. Meanwhile the noise of the combat brought a crowd of armed men out of the coffee-room, and also awoke Savrimovitch and Mouravioff, who hurried to my assistance.

"Hulloh !" said Mouravioff, rather sarcastically, " do English sailors fight with knapsacks as well as cutlasses?"

" Yes," replied I, triumphantly ; " they always knock their enemies over, and are not very particular how they do it ! "

Savrimovitch strode up to my late opponent, whose name, by the way, was Pauloff, and gave him a sharp reprimand for molesting me. Pauloff replied by a defiant scowl, and began haranguing the soldiers and detailing his grievances to them, and some seemed half disposed to take his part. Savrimovitch, however, soon put an end to the quarrel. Speaking in a loud, authoritative tone, he ordered the soldiers to arrest that " drunken fellow" (pointing to Pauloff) " for assaulting this good English doctor."

My friend's fine presence and commanding manner acted like magic on the Servians. The infuriated Pauloff was collared, and in spite of his frantic struggles and remonstrances, marched off to the guard-room. Peace being thus restored, the soldiers cleared out of the room again, we returned to our beds, and slept tranquilly the rest of the night.

CHAPTER XI.

THE first thing next morning, we went to the market-place in quest of our lost conveyance. To our great delight we found it, but just on the point of starting without us. Our friends welcomed us with a cheer, and the caravan pulled up whilst we took our places. Then we bid good-bye to Paratchin, and trundled off towards the front again. It was a lovely morning, and we were all in excellent spirits, for we expected to reach Deligrad early in the evening. We whiled away the time in planning all sorts of desperate expeditions and adventures.

Savrimovitch proposed that we should provide ourselves with horses, and act as mounted scouts—for the army—whenever an opportunity offered. I suggested that we should imitate the example of Athos, Porthos, and D'Arlagnan of the Mousquetaires, provision a cottage in the midst of the Turkish lines, and defend it for six months against the whole of the hostile army. My suggestion was received with shouts of approving laughter. Mouravioff patted me on the back, and said I was undoubtedly a military genius of the highest order.

The handsome Savrimovitch said, with a smile, "But supposing they bring cannon against your cottage!" to which I replied, that our defence then would be all the more creditable. He smiled again, and shaking me warmly by the hand, said that I was a "brave!"

When we were still some distance from Deligrad, we heard the distant booming of cannon for the first time. This excited us all so much, that we gave a loud cheer, which was caught up by our friends in the other waggons, and the drivers whipped up their tired horses, and we bounded along in fine style. Soon after this a party of horsemen approached us, led by an officer in whom I recognised, to my surprise, the bald-headed Russian I had met at the restaurant with Savrimovitch.

"See," said Mouravioff, "here comes the prince!"

"The prince!" said I, in astonishment, "what prince?"

"Why, Prince Obolenski, of course."

"You don't mean to say," said I, "that that gentleman is a prince?"

"Certainly I do!"

"Goodness me!" I exclaimed in dismay; "I trust he was not offended at the cool way in which I spoke to him."

"Not he," replied Savrimovitch, "he is very good-natured."

Meanwhile the *cortège* had come up to the leading waggon, which stopped, and its occupants stood up and saluted the prince.

As he approached us, we did the same.

The prince reined up at our waggon, and shook hands very kindly with all three of us.

" Ah, M. Wright," said he, " I am very pleased to see you. I have been talking about you to Dr. Gigglei-vitch."

" Dr. Giggleivitch ? " repeated I, in alarm.

" Yes," rejoined the Prince, " Yermaylaff Giggleivitch. We travelled from Semendria together. Do you know him? "

" Well," said I, " I cannot exactly say that I know him, but I met him once under rather embarrassing circumstances ; " and I narrated my little adventure with him at Belgrade.

. The prince laughed heartily, and then said, " That explains it all. Yermaylaff Giggleivitch looked anything but pleased when I told him you were coming, and absolutely refused to give you a surgeon's commission as surgeon under him " (I looked very blank at this), " but you need not let that trouble you. I can offer you, if you like, the rank of lieutenant in one of our best brigades here,—the Medvedovski's Brigade,—where you will have plenty of opportunities both of practising your profession and of fighting."

I was overwhelmed with joy and gratitude at this. Even had he given me the chance, I doubt whether I could have found words in which to thank him ; but without waiting, he shook hands with us again, and trotted off with his followers.

When we reached the camp we were directed to head-quarters, which were held at a large cottage close to the road. We left our waggons and formed into line. Presently three or four officers came out; we all stood at attention. I was particularly anxious to create a good impression, and threw my shoulders well back and held myself as rigidly as possible.

"That officer with the imperial moustache and beard is General Tchernaieff," said Savrimovitch to me in a whisper. Without turning my head, I looked at this renowned soldier out of the corners of my eyes with greater interest.

Before coming to us, the general spoke to two or three men who were standing near in a group.

"By Jove," continued Savrimovitch, still whispering, "the general's in a great rage about something ! Do you notice the way in which he puffs out his cheeks and sucks them in again ? He always does that when he's angry. I expect these men are asking for leave of absence, a thing he hates."

The general, who was a sallow-faced man of medium height, and nowise remarkable in personal appearance, was indeed puffing out his cheeks in a very odd manner. Presently, and without returning their salute, he turned his back on the unfortunates who had excited his wrath, and came towards us.

"If he is pleased with us," said Savrimovitch, "he will beat a kind of devil's tattoo with his finger against the side of his leg."

GENERAL TCHERNAIEFF, FROM A PHOTOGRAPH BY
VOVANOVITCH OF BELGRADE.

To face p. 102.]

I watched him carefully as he walked deliberately up
to our line, and noticed, first, the angry shade fade away
from his face. As he passed from man to man and
asked each one where he came from and what service he
had seen, his fingers began to play at first slowly, then
more quickly, and finally, when he spoke to Savrimovitch,
his satisfaction appeared to reach its climax. He looked
rather doubtfully at me, and I thought I could discern
just the suspicion of an inflation of the cheeks when he
heard I was an Englishman ; but as I answered all his
questions satisfactorily, this indication of displeasure
passed away, and before he left me, I had the satisfaction
of seeing his fingers gently ambling up and down his
continuations.

Four of us—namely Savrimovitch, Mouravioff, the big
dragoon officer who gave me the boots, and whose name
was Nicolaitch, and myself—were told that we were to join
the Medvedovski Brigade, so without losing time we set
out for its headquarters.

Deligrad itself is—or rather was at that time—an
insignificant hamlet, numbering a normal population of
perhaps a couple of hundred, but the camp, which
surrounded it on all sides, contained from thirty to
forty thousand men. The position was naturally strong,
and had been fortified by trenches, rifle pits, and earth-
works, mounting upwards of one hundred guns of every
calibre and of all kinds. There were old smooth bores
and new Krupps, little six pounders and huge sixty
pounders. The plain in front of the camp was, moreover,

studded with little pits containing sharp stakes for the benefit of the enemy's cavalry. The trees, too, in the vicinity had been felled, stripped of their leaves and twigs, and, with their branches sharpened, disposed as an abattis to further hamper the movements of an attacking force.

The position of the Medvedovski Brigade lay about half a mile to the right and rear of the general's head-quarters.

The Medvedovski Brigade—so called from its commander, Colonel Medvedovski, an officer of the Russian Imperial Guard—was also known as the Russian Brigade, from the nationality of many of its officers.

Colonel Medvedovski, a dark, stern-looking man, with a short, well-trimmed moustache and beard, bade us welcome to his brigade in a short, and doubtless pithy, oration in Russian, of which, unfortunately, I failed to understand a single word.

"You are a medical student!" said the colonel to me in French, at the end of his harangue.

" I am, sir," replied I.

" May I ask why you elect to serve as a combatant instead of following up your own profession ? "

" Because I wish to see some fighting, sir."

The colonel gave me a keen glance, and said, with a smile,—

" You are evidently an original, sir. May I trouble you to hand me your passport and other papers ? Thank you ; you must entrust them to my keeping until you leave the camp. Do not think, sir, that we suspect your *bona fides* in any way ; we adopt the same precaution with all volunteers coming here. Meantime, I am very glad to receive an Englishman into my brigade, and if I can be of any service to you whilst you are with us, you have but to speak to me, and I will do what I can for you."

Standing behind the colonel was a singular-looking individual, apparently about thirty-five years of age. His hair was of an extremely light colour, his complexion florid and weather-beaten. He had a feeble white moustache, and a little tuft of hair on either side of his chin, one of which was bright red, the other of a pale straw-colour. His features were flat, his right eye grey, and his left blue. In spite of the peculiarity of his appearance, his expression was pleasing.

This was Count Réné, who had the reputation of being one of the bravest of all the gallant Russians then in Servia.

I had just thanked Colonel Medvedovski for his kindness, and was turning to leave the tent with my companions, when Count Réné came up to me and shook me by the hand.

"You are to join my battalion—the fourth. Permit me to offer you a hearty welcome to it. You are the only Englishman in the whole brigade, therefore I shall expect great things of you, for I have heard much of English courage ! "

The count's words set my ambition in a blaze ; my

7

heart beat wildly, and I felt the blood mount to my face. I, however, restrained my feelings until I had bid him adieu, and merely replied that I should be proud and happy to do the best I could for the honour of the battalion. I inwardly resolved, however, to do something desperately valiant to maintain my reputation as a brave Englishman. The idea that occurred to me at the moment was to send a challenge to the officers of the Turkish army, defying any of them to meet me in single combat. With a feeling of proud elation, I imagined myself posing in the hanging-guard attitude before the assembled Servian and Turkish hosts, and after a terrible encounter vanquishing the hostile champion, and then saving his life by a brilliant surgical operation. The fame of my glorious deeds, I rapturously thought, would not be confined to Servia, but would extend all over Europe to England—and then, who knows what might happen? Many a man has passed along a less creditable avenue to Royal patronage! I rubbed my hands, and laughed with glee at the thought!

"Why, how now, M. Wright," said Savrimovitch, banteringly, "what are you laughing at? Have you been drinking champagne on the sly?"

"No," replied I, somewhat vexed that my elation should be deemed of the vinous sort; "I am simply very glad that we shall so soon have an opportunity of distinguishing ourselves."

"Pooh, is that all?" said Savrimovitch. "I thought

you were a little bit screwed, and was hoping you had brought a bottle or two of Heidsick with you."

" I daresay, M. Wright, that you will not feel quite so festive when you really have seen some fighting," said Mouravioff, dryly.

CHAPTER XII.

THE brigade of which I was now a member was about 2,000 strong, and was encamped on what had once been a field of maize. Here and there lines of stiff, stubbly stumps still stuck out of the ground. The camp was very picturesque. It was composed of hundreds of booths, arranged in rows, and intersected at regular intervals by broad thoroughfares. These booths were ingeniously constructed of green boughs, interlaced, and supported by one or two stout upright pieces of timber. Some of them were like little huts, and afforded very complete shelter, and others were entirely opened on one side, like arbours, and to one of these latter we were directed. It already contained two occupants,—Count Tiesenhausen and Baron Kleist —both of them Courlanders. They proved to be old acquaintances of Savrimovitch and Mouravioff, to whom they gave a very warm and hearty welcome. They also received Nicolaitch and myself very politely, and we were soon all on the very best of terms. Count Tiesenhausen was a handsome, blonde little man, who encased his legs in a huge pair of cavalry boots, and smothered his face under a Servian military cap, which was many sizes

too large for him, and came down to his eyes and brows.
Baron Kleist, a tall, gaunt man, with very strongly-
marked aquiline features, and a sandy-coloured beard
and moustache, suffered a good deal from ague, and
always wore an overcoat with its collar turned up. He
divided his spare time between sleeping and smoking,
and for the greater part of it I think he was to be seen
squatted on his heels puffing at a cigarette. But both
Kleist and Tiesenhausen were brave soldiers, and amiable and accomplished gentlemen.

It was now late in the afternoon. We had eaten
nothing but a biscuit or two and a few grapes since we
left Paratchin. We were glad, therefore, when the count
summoned our mess servant, who was quite a character in
his way, to prepare supper. Imagine a funny mannikin,
with a pair of very roguish-looking, twinkling black eyes,
the smallest and snubbiest of small snub noses, and a
gigantic pair of moustaches. The creature, whose name
was Jenko, at once cut some thick slices from a large
piece of mutton, put them on a long spit, and proceeded
to grill them over a large wood fire which smouldered
in front of our hut.

We all lent a willing hand in one way or another.
Tiesenhausen and Mouravioff walked over to Deligrad,
and bought some wine and spirits at one of the numerous provision stalls which had sprung up round the
camp; Nicolaitch occupied himself in superintending
the baking of some potatoes; Kleist roasted coffee-
berries in a frying-pan; and Savrimovitch and I pounded

the same, he with the butt end of his revolver, and I
with the heel of a drinking horn.   When we had finished
breaking up the coffee-berries, we put the fragments into
a pot containing about half a gallon of water.   The
resulting fluid was of a pale straw colour, and tasted
very strongly of wood and smoke, and feebly, very
feebly, of coffee.   The meat was terribly tough, having
been killed that morning, and the black commissariat
bread of the consistency of putty, and about as digestible.   Still, in spite of these little drawbacks, we all ate
very heartily, and formed an exceedingly merry little
party.   As the evening advanced and the stars began to
twinkle overhead, hundreds of huge fires were lit throughout the camp, round which groups of armed men sat or
reclined, their faces and accoutrements, illumined with
vivid distinctness by the leaping flames.   I looked with
delight on the scene, and said to myself, " Yes, this is
real warfare, and no mistake about it ! "

Whilst indulging in warlike musing, a voice struck my
ear so singularly like that of Marie Miloikovitch that
it sent a thrill right through me.   It came from a group
of three officers who were walking towards our hut.   I
could not make out their faces in the gloom, until the
light of the fire fell on them.   Then I saw with amazement that one bore so astonishing a resemblance to the
charming Bulgarian who had captivated my heart at
Semendria, that I started and exclaimed, " Hulloh ! "

All three turned their faces towards me, and I fancied
that the young officer who was so like Marie changed

SERVIAN CAMP KITCHEN.

To face p. 110.]

colour when he saw me. But it might have been only my fancy, or a fitful shadow cast by the flickering flames. Anyway, they resumed their conversation, and passed on without taking further notice.

The likeness was most amazing.

"Still," thought I, "I must be mistaken. It is all but impossible that the beautiful and accomplished Marie should have cast aside the feelings of her sex and donned a soldier's uniform."

Then I recalled her strange conduct during our memorable walk at Semendria when she discharged my revolver, and I came to the conclusion that it might be she after all. I was agitated and perplexed, and resolved to follow the cause of my mental confusion and ask if he was Marie, and had actually started off, when the absurdity of putting such a question to a man brought me back to my senses—and—our fireside.

"Why! what's the matter with you, M. Wright?" said Savrimovitch, slapping me on the back. "You're not ill, I hope?"

"Ill," replied I, looking at him vacantly; "no, I'm not ill!"

"I'm glad to hear that," said my friend, "for you've been muttering to yourself, starting and staring about you, like a man with delirium tremens, for the last fifteen minutes. Come to the hut, and be a little more sociable."

At ten o'clock we all turned in for the night ; *i.e.*, we lay down on the ground in the clothes we wore. I had no overcoat, so Savrimovitch good-naturedly insisted on spreading a portion of his over me.

My companions were soon fast asleep, but the novelty of the situation and the exciting events of the day— especially the incident I have just described—kept me awake a long time, and when at length I fell asleep my rest was disturbed by all kinds of strange dreams.

The bugle roused us next morning at half-past five, and in a few minutes we were all wide awake and astir. Most of the Servian bugle calls are tuneful,—the *réveille* especially. It begins with a quick and lively strain, and ends with a long, melancholy wail. Half-a-dozen buglers were sounding it in different parts of the camp, so that the whole air was ringing with melodious and inspiriting sounds. Though I got up with as much show of alacrity as the others, I felt both stiff and chilly, for the morning was cold and the dew falling heavily. I excited some surprise and laughter by stripping to the waist to wash myself. The mannikin, Jenko, could not understand the proceeding at all.

When I shouted to him for " voda " (water) he brought some in an earthenware pitcher of classical shape, and poured about ten drops on to my hand.

" What's the good of that, you little duffer ? " said I. " I want you to pour some over my head and back," and stooping down, I motioned to him to do so.

With a nod and smile of intelligence, the little man dropped about four minims more on to my back, and then turned to depart. I stopped him angrily, and appealed to Mouravioff, who was standing near, to explain to him what I wanted.

"I think Jenko understands what you want, M. Wright, but our water supply is brought from some distance, and we are consequently compelled to use it as sparingly as possible."

"Good gracious me!" said I in dismay; "but we shall get very dirty if we are allowed only fourteen minims of water per diem for our ablutions!"

"My dear M. Wright, that is one of the disagreeable exigencies of campaigning. In Turkestan I have been very thankful sometimes to have enough water to drink."

"And I've wasted my fourteen minims!" said I, with a groan.

"Oh, well!" laughed Count Tiesenhausen, who just then came up to us barefooted, with his top boots under his arm, "I daresay Jenko can find a drop or two more at the bottom of his pitcher!"

The imp, Jenko, did contrive to squeeze out about a couple of scruples more, and these I caught on a corner of my pocket-handkerchief, and with it polished up my visage as well as I could. At about six o'clock we sat down to a breakfast of hot coffee-water (I won't tell a falsehood and call it coffee!), black bread, grilled mutton, biscuits, and sheep's-milk cheese. This last was white, friable, and rather palatable, though intensely salt.

At seven the whole battalion turned out for drill. The men were a motley crew. They had no uniforms, and every one was dressed in the costume of the class

to which he belonged.   At first I drilled in the ranks,
partly because I thought I should so learn the words of
command,   and   partly   *pour   encourager   les   autres.*
On this occasion I recollect that my right-hand man
was a dapper little patriot, in a grey civilian suit, while
my left-hand man was a huge, stupid-looking peasant,
wearing a short jacket over a loose linen garment, bound
round the waist by a broad sash, baggy knickerbocker
trousers, and a fez without a tassel.   I wore my black
volunteer suit.

Nearly all the Russian officers had bought regular
military uniforms at Belgrade.

About a fortnight after my arrival, however, at the
camp, Prince Obolenski generously supplied the whole
brigade with a smart, serviceable uniform and overcoat
at his own expense.

Had I known the peril of drilling in the ranks with
raw recruits, I think my zeal, great as it was, would not
have nerved me to undergo such a trial.

The drill was of the most elementary description.
We were simply put through our facings ; made to stand
at attention, present, shoulder, slope, and trail arms,
and form fours, but everything was very badly done.

This is not to be wondered at, for the men had been
hurried into the ranks from the desk and the plough,
but I was not prepared for the extent of their ignorance.
To make matters worse, the bayonets remained fixed
throughout the drill, and some of the recruits, in spite
of orders to the contrary, had their rifles loaded—notably

the burly idiot on my left. This interesting individual distinguished himself by doing everything wrong. At the word "Attention!" he grounded his rifle with horrible force on my toes; in forming fours he was my rear rank man, and gave me a nasty prod in the back with his bayonet, and had it not providentially struck against my waist belt, the wound might have been serious. As it was, I got off with a painful scratch, and finally the charge in his rifle exploded, and was within an ace of blowing my head off. This was the climax. Count Tiesenhausen sternly ordered him to fall out of the ranks, gave him a good cuffing, which he took with stolid meekness, and put him under arrest. I was afterwards told that he and two or three other dangerous incompetents had been relegated to the awkward squad.

After drill, Savrimovitch and Count Tiesenhausen introduced me to several officers of the battalion, who invited us to dine with them. We accepted the invitation, and accompanied them to their quarters, which were in what had once been a farmyard.

CHAPTER XIII.

THIS farmyard was surrounded by a low wall and had a wide entrance, on either side of which stood a wooden post. To each of these was tied a man, stripped to the waist, and bound hand and foot, with a placard hanging from his neck, on which was written a sentence in Servian characters.

"Hulloh!" said I, "what is the meaning of this?"

"One of them has been guilty of stealing, the other of gross insubordination," said one of our hosts, Major Bernadski, a fine-looking old Russian, "and they are to be flogged this evening."

I asked if they were Russians or Servians.

"The thief, I am sorry to say, is a Russian, the other is a Sclav. Some of our men are very angry that a Russian should be treated like that, and have asked me to intercede with the colonel for him. But I shall do nothing of the kind; the rascal deserves his sentence well. Did you ever see such a villainous face?"

Looking closely at the unhappy man, I recognised, to my unbounded astonishment, my acquaintance, Pauloff, the man whom I had vanquished in the bedroom at Paratchin a day or two before. He evidently recognised me, too, for he darted a very evil look at me out of his wicked little eyes.

I felt so sorry for the poor fellow that I persuaded Savrimovitch and Count Tiesenhausen to try to get his sentence remitted. I am happy to say their intercession proved so far successful, that he escaped the flogging.

Dinner that night was quite a banquet. We had mutton broth, beef tea, made with Liebig's Extract, grilled and haricot mutton, potatoes and rice, wine and smoked coffee-water—the latter, by the way, tasting a little more of coffee, and a little less of smoke, than that of our own manufacture.

After dinner we disposed ourselves comfortably on the straw with which the yard was littered, filled our glasses, lit our cigarettes, and began to chat.

"Pardon me for asking you such a question, M. Wright," said Bernadski, politely clinking his glass against mine, "but what will you do when Russia declares war against England?"

"I would ask the general for a flag of truce, and go over to the Turks," replied I.

The Russians laughed.

"Our general would never allow you to do that, after having seen our positions. He would probably send you to Belgrade, and detain you there on parole," said one of them.

"Well, I should think that very shabby treatment," said I, rather indignantly; "but it is to be hoped that there will be no necessity for war between our countries."

"It is to be hoped not; still a war with England would be very popular with us, because your government so openly support our enemies the Turks!"

"What will England do when we have conquered India?" said Baron Kleist, solemnly, from behind his rampart of coat collar, and blowing at the same time a huge cloud of tobacco smoke from his nostrils.

"Russia never *will* conquer India," replied I, amused at his cool cheek.

"What! Do you mean to say they don't believe in England that we are to get India?" said Bernadski.

"Certainly!" said I. "We don't doubt that you would like to get India, but we are quite sure that you will never have it."

"Well," said Bernadski, "you must be either blind or infatuated, that is all I can say. Do you not see how rapidly we are approaching your frontiers?"

"Yes, we notice that," replied I.

"Then what is there to prevent us from attacking you and driving you out, as soon as we are ready?" said the Russian.

"Simply the fact that you are not, and never will be, strong enough."

My reply was received with a shout of laughter.

"Not strong enough!" said Bernadski, echoing my words as if he had not heard them aright.

"No, not strong enough," repeated I. "I doubt if you would be able to conquer and hold Afghanistan, much less India."

Another shout of laughter followed this reply.

" Why," said Mouravioff, confidently, " I would undertake to conquer Afghanistan with one regiment of infantry
and a single squadron of Cossacks ; and give me 20,000
of my old Khivan comrades, I would undertake to make
the whole of India mine."

" And I am equally willing to undertake," said I
warmly, " that if you had ten, or even twenty times the
number of men you mention, you would not succeed,
for the whole manhood of England would rise in arms to
prevent you ! "

" M. Wright," said Baron Kleist, very solemnly
indeed, " if you do not believe that we are to conquer
India, you cannot believe in the Bible ! "

" I believe in the Bible," said I, " but I cannot see
what that has to do with a Russian conquest of India."

" I will tell you," replied the baron. " In the
eleventh chapter of Daniel it says that the king of the
north shall fight against the king of the south, and shall
conquer him, and take his possessions and the rich and
glorious land from him. Now, you cannot deny that
Russia, the great northern power, is the king of the
north, and England, with India, is the king of the south.
Ergo, we shall conquer you, and take India, the rich and
glorious land referred to, from you. Is not that clear
enough ? "

The Russians greeted the baron's rendering of this
portion of the Scriptures with loud applause, and turned
to me for my reply.

I said that if the prophecy had any reference to the conquest of India, it had probably been fulfilled when England conquered India. At that time, England might well claim to be the king of the north and India the king of the south.

My answer was received with a groan of disapprobation, and one of my audience said that my interpretation of the policy was a very strained one.

" Sir," said another officer, "the possession of India is part of Russia's destiny !"

" How so ? " I asked.

" Russia, at present," said he, " is not a rich nation ; it is absolutely necessary for her to acquire wealth. India, with her incalculable treasures, offers herself an easy prey to us, therefore we shall take her."

" Your reason does not seem to be a very good one, and, moreover, leads you to a wrong conclusion," said I, enthusiastically; " for I am convinced that it is England's destiny to civilize and Christianize India, and so long as we do our duty by her, so long shall we keep her. It is quite possible, I admit, that we may not have done all that we might in this direction, but I think that we have done much more than you or any of the other powers would have done under the circumstances."

" Well, well, my dear sir," said M. Bernadski, giving me a pat on the back, " wait a bit, and we shall see ! "

" Yes," said I, " we shall see ! "

On the way back to our quarters I mentioned to Savrimovitch and Count Tiesenhausen my idea of sending a challenge to the Turkish officers, but they told me that my scheme was out of the question, and impracticable ; at which I was greatly disappointed. I was somewhat comforted, however, when they told me that we should soon be attacking the Turks, and that then I should not be wanting in opportunities in which to display my courage.

That night I lay awake for a long time thinking over different schemes for distinguishing myself. I was not satisfied with the prospect of merely taking part in a general engagement.

"Thousands and thousands of men," thought I, " will do the same, and I shall be no more distinguished than they. No," I argued, " as I am the only Englishman in the brigade, it behoves me to perform some remarkable feat ! "

But what on earth this was to be I could not, for a long time, conceive. Suddenly, I remembered my plan of occupying a cottage in the Turkish lines.

" I'll propose that to Savrimovitch and Mouravioff to-morrow. Hurrah ! " and I was meditating with great delight on this magnificent and warlike adventure when Morpheus slyly stole me away from the contemplation of Mars, and dropped me into the land of dreams. In other words, I fell asleep.

The next morning I suggested to Savrimovitch that he and I should go on a reconnoitring expedition, and if we found a suitable cottage within the enemy's lines, or within a reasonable distance of them, we should occupy it forthwith.

8

Savrimovitch talked the matter over with Mouravioff, and the latter said he would very much like to accompany us in the reconnoitring expedition, but he feared that if we did occupy a cottage in the Turkish lines the occupation would be permanent.

"No, no," said I, "there's no object in our permanently occupying the place; six months will be quite long enough."

Both my friends, for no reason that I could see, laughed heartily at this, and Mouravioff said that I was indeed a remarkable military genius; at which I felt flattered, although I tried not to show it. As soon as we had breakfasted, we asked Count Réné's leave to go on our reconnoitring expedition; but he, after giving us a kindly greeting, referred us to Colonel Medvedovski. We accordingly repaired to our brigadier's quarters, and found him standing in front of his tent, perusing some despatches.

"Well, gentlemen," said he, returning our salute, "what can I do for you?"

"We wish for a day's leave of absence from the camp, sir. We want to see the enemy's lines!" said Savrimovitch.

"You want to go on a reconnoitring expedition, in fact," observed the colonel.

"Precisely so, sir," said Savrimovitch.

"Then I am sorry to say I cannot give you leave. However," continued he, seeing our disappointment, "I want some letters conveyed to the commander of the Krusevac Brigade, which is stationed at Jubovac, close to the Turkish position. If you like to take them you will have an opportunity of seeing something of the enemy, only mind you don't get into any mischief. If you will be good enough to come into my tent for a minute I will give you the documents.

We followed 'him into his tent, which, by the way, was the only bit of canvas in the whole of our camp. Colonel Medvedovski desired us to be seated, pointing to some boxes and camp stools, offered us some wine, and then rapidly penned and handed us a note, which, together with a bundle of papers, he asked us to give to Colonel Philipovitch.

"Jubovac," said he, "is nearly twenty miles from here, so you shall have a waggon." Turning to an orderly who stood by the door of the tent, he said some words to him in Russian. The man immediately disappeared : then he wished us "good day !" and told us the waggon would be at our quarters in a few minutes.

We thanked the colonel heartily, and hurried back again to our hut, our hearts beating high with excitement and pleasure.

Our comrades were not a little jealous when they learned that we were going to Jubovac. They, however, good-naturedly wished us *bon voyage* and a pleasant time of it. We took with us a supply of biscuits, some Liebig's Extract, some spirits and water, our revolvers, a rifle apiece, and some ammunition. My friends tried to dissuade me from taking my cutlass with me, saying it would be a useless encumbrance, but I really could not bear to part with it.

How could I figure in the hanging-guard position, thought I, without a cutlass ?

I also took with me a few drugs, some lint, bandages, etc., and a small amputating case. As I felt the edge of the knives, I reflected complacently on the inestimable advantages humanity derives from surgical science. The wounded Turk, said I to myself, that falls into my hands may well consider himself a fortunate individual ! My incisions shall be boldly and skilfully made, and I flatter myself that his stumps will be perfect pictures !

Scarcely were our preparations completed when the waggon came rumbling up, and bidding our friends *au revoir*, we got into it, and in another minute were being jolted over the uneven ground *en route* for Jubovac.

We had a good driver, a good horse, a good road, a beautiful day, and lovely scenery. It is not surprising, therefore, that we were as jovial as we could be. Some distance from Deligrad we crossed the Morava by a bridge of boats. We passed several inns, but were so eager to push on that we would not stop until we had covered about twelve miles. Then, as the horse began to show signs of fatigue, we halted at a little wayside place, gave him a feed and a drink, of which he was badly in want, as the sun was terrifically hot, and partook of a little refreshment ourselves.

About one o'clock we were off again. We had gone

a considerable distance further on our way, when we suddenly heard the distant report of a rifle, then another, and another, then a volley, followed by a smart and continuous fusillade. Excited beyond measure by these martial sounds, we made our driver urge on the horse to its utmost speed, and eagerly inspected our weapons, to see that they were in readiness. As we hurried along, the din was increased by the boom of cannon. The sound seemed to come from our left front, but partly from the hilly nature of the ground, and partly from the distance, we failed to see even the smoke of the firing. Presently we were challenged by a sentinel, and coming to a standstill were surrounded by an armed party, and conducted into the camp of the Krusevac Brigade. Here we found all the men under arms.

As we drove past their ranks, Colonel Philipovitch, the commanding officer of the brigade, rode up. He was a tall, stout man, with a stubbly ginger-coloured moustache and beard, and a very good-natured face. A Servian, and a native of Belgrade in the piping times of peace, he carried out a flourishing business as general merchant, which probably accounted for his sleek and comfortable appearance, and now at the call of duty he had donned the " horrid panoply of war," and was transformed into a stout—a very stout—soldier. His cap, which was far too small for him, was cocked very much on one side of his head, and between his lips he held a cigarette, at which he sucked with a smacking noise. As he read the letters we gave him, he would

look at us ever and anon with a friendly smile and a
nod, and then go on with his reading again. All at
once he flung the reins to one of the soldiers, and
scrambling out of his saddle with a considerable amount
of agility for his size, shouted out,—

"Ah! an Englishman! an Englishman!" and rushed
up to us with outstretched arms. "Which, which,"
said he, with affectionate eagerness, "is the Englishman?
Which is my English brother?"

I modestly replied that I was an Englishman.

Scarcely were the words out of my mouth, when I
was enveloped in his huge embrace, and I verily believe
he would have kissed me had I not averted my face.

Such was the energy of his greeting that he turned
me round, so that, on looking over his shoulder, I
found myself facing my friends. I could not resist
the temptation of improving the situation and of making
a really striking tableau, so I wagged my head about
behind the back of the all-unconscious colonel, and
indulged in a few of my choicest grimaces, with the
effect of sending his staff and Savrimovitch and
Mouravioff into convulsions of laughter. I blamed
myself very much afterwards for this ill-timed jesting,
of which, luckily, Colonel Philipovitch remained in
entire ignorance.

We then asked the cause of the firing.

"General Horvatovics (Horvatovitch) has been making
a reconnaissance of the enemy's position at Greviatz,"
said one of the officers.

COLONEL PHILIPOVITCH WITH HIS LUNCH IN HIS BREECHES' POCKET.

To face p. 126.]

"How far off is that?" we asked.

"Four miles," was the reply.

"Then you will not have any fighting to-day," said Savrimovitch, in a tone of disappointment.

"No, unless they attack us, which is not likely, as we are very strong here," said the officer.

"Captain Ilia Ilianovitch, dismiss the men. There is no occasion for us to remain longer under arms," exclaimed the colonel; then turning to us, he added, "Now, my friends, come to my quarters and have some dinner with me, for I am sure you must be hungry."

We readily accepted this hospitable invitation, and following our host into his tent, soon had the satisfaction of seeing a magnificent banquet spread before us. It was very obvious, that even in the midst of the horrors of war the gallant colonel did not forget the creature comforts of peace. There was a cold fowl, some pork cutlets, a ham, sardines, caviare, and oh, ye gods! a couple of Rehoboams of champagne. Our long and dusty drive gave zest to our appetites.

Colonel Philipovitch, moreover, was an excellent host, and took care that we did ample justice to his hospitality; he would not suffer our glasses to remain empty for a moment, and when at length our appetites were stayed he produced cigars, and we enjoyed a blissful half-hour's smoke.

"Colonel," said Savrimovitch, when he was half through his cigar, "how far off is the enemy from here?"

" Well," said Philipovitch, " his nearest pickets are stationed about a mile off, and he is in force on a range of hills about a mile further back. I will show you his batteries if you like, gentlemen."

We replied eagerly that we should like to see them, so our host rose, took down a field-glass that hung from the tent-post, and asking us to accompany him, walked out.

The camp of the Krusevac Brigade was situated on the side of a hill, to the brow of which the stout colonel laboriously, and with much puffing and groan_ing, endeavoured to mount. When at length we reached the top, we saw beneath us a valley about three thousand yards in breadth, bounded on the opposite side by a range of hills similar to the one we stood on. The intervening space was, for the most part, covered with forest.

" There," said he, pointing across the valley to one of the opposite hills,—" there are the Turkish batteries ! "

The batteries were so cleverly masked that at first I could not make out where they were, but after a long look with the glass I succeeded in discerning them.

"Which position is the best," said I, " ours or theirs ? "

" Theirs," said Savrimovitch ; " it commands this altogether. By Jove ! they are firing at us ; look there !"

Just as he spoke a puff of white smoke leapt forth from the battery, and the next moment I heard, for the first time in my life, the screaming of a shell as it whistled through the air.

'Lie down, boys!'" sung out Colonel Philipovitch, throwing himself down on the ground.

The noise of the shell was extremely disagreeable, and I felt a strong inclination to follow the colonel's example, but as Savrimovitch and Mouravioff refused to budge, I felt bound to remain standing as well. The missile, luckily, went over our heads, and exploded with a loud but harmless crash a good way behind us.

"Foolish boys, foolish boys!" said the colonel, as he got up again; "you are not wise; you want to be killed for nothing! Ah, ah! I am angry with you!" and he shook his head reproachfully at us, and then patted us affectionately on the back. Probably disgusted with the failure of his shot, the enemy did not fire at us again, and we continued our survey without further molestation.

About half a mile from the foot of the hill was a clearing of about four hundred acres in extent. In this secluded spot a group of cottages had stood before the war; now, only, one remained intact, the others having been knocked into shapeless heaps of ruins. The only signs of life that we could see were two or three curling wreaths of smoke that ascended from the outskirt of the forest on the other side of the clearing.

"That smoke," said Colonel Philipovitch, "comes from the Turkish outposts in the forest."

The sight of the ruins and the horrible noise made by the shell in its flight and explosion had greatly shaken my faith in the feasibility of a six months' occupation of a cottage in the Turkish lines, but I was ashamed to withdraw from my proposal, so pointing to the little building in the clearing, I proposed that we should straightway occupy it. My two friends nodded and smiled, and addressing Colonel Philipovitch, informed him of our wish.

For a long time our kind-hearted host would not hear of it.

"We should be going," he said, "to certain death. The Turks would infallibly cut us to pieces;" and he tried to frighten us by relating, with rolling eyes and working fingers, stories of the atrocities committed by Bashi-Bazouks,—that they gave no quarter, sparing neither age nor sex, and that one of their favourite methods of disposing of prisoners was to chop them into little bits and afterwards roast them alive.

We were, however, resolute, and succeeded at last in gaining the colonel's permission to pass a night in the cottage.

I did not feel so joyful and enthusiastic as I ought to have done; possibly the blood-curdling earnestness with which Colonel Philipovitch had alluded to the black doings of the bloodthirsty Bashi-Bazouks had acted as a damper to my spirits. Still I contrived to assume an appearance of considerable glee and martial alacrity, and proposed in a frisky tone that we should start at once.

The stout colonel, however, insisted that we should

drink a farewell glass with him, and lay in a stock of provisions.

"If you *must* go," said he, sadly, "take plenty to eat and drink with you. It is hard," and here he spoke with an air of the profoundest conviction, "to be valiant and fight well on an empty stomach."

We all agreed that there was much sense in what he said, and accompanying him to his quarters, we gratefully accepted at his hands a bottle of raki, some cold meat, bread, a tin of *pâté de foie gras*, and a bundle of cigars.

It was about four o'clock when we set out. Colonel Philipovitch walked a short distance, and showed us a zigzag trench, probably part of a rifle-pit, which ran down the hill to the outskirts of the forest.

"Walk down that trench, dear friends," said he, embracing us as affectionately as if he had known us for twenty years, "and you are less likely to be seen by the Turks. I do wish you would let me dissuade you from going on this mad errand, but I see it is no use talking to you about it. Well, well. I only hope you'll come to no harm, and mind, if you are found out, to make at once for the trench, and I will do what I can for you. Good-bye !"

"Good-bye, colonel !" we shouted as we leaped into the trench.

He waved his hand, and for some seconds stood gazing at us with an expression of deep concern in his fat but pleasant face ; then a sudden turn in our pathway hid him from our view.

CHAPTER XIV.

WE walked down the steep and narrow path in single file. Mouravioff led the way, Savrimovitch came next, and I brought up the rear. We carried our loaded rifles in our hands, unfastened our revolver cases, and brought them well round to the front of our belts, in order to be handy, if required. None of us felt much inclined to talk, so that for some distance the only sounds we heard were the snapping of twigs under our feet, the hum of insects, and the note of birds in the woods hard by.

" How is it," said I all at once to Savrimovitch, " that the Turks don't put their outpost into that comfortable little cottage instead of keeping them in the open air ? "

" For the very simple reason," replied he, " that we should knock it into pieces in two minutes with our cannon."

" Oh ! " said I, mentally casting a glance at my scheme of a six months' occupation, to which this reply dealt a staggering blow.

" And similarly," continued he, " the Turkish guns render it impossible for us to occupy it openly."

My favourite plan was now completely demolished and pulverised.

On emerging from the trench, we entered the forest which clothed the hill on this side right down to its base, and extended as far as the heights occupied by the Turks. A few minutes' brisk walking under the trees, whose shade gave welcome relief from the burning sun, brought us to the edge of the clearing, and within two hundred yards of the cottage. We now walked from our cover, and scanned the forest held by the enemy.

Everything was as still as death. We held brief discussions whether one of us should enter it first, or all three advance together. We decided upon the latter course. We left the shadow of the trees, therefore, and walking boldly across the clearing got to the cottage without being perceived by the enemy.

The place looked cheerless and uninviting. The walls were of hardened mud, and a roughly-constructed door swung loosely on its hinges, and the thatched roof was in a dilapidated condition. There were but two rooms, each with a small aperture for a window. The room in the front of the hovel had apparently been used as a kitchen, and in it we found a large heap of grain, a three-legged milking stool, and the fragment of a distaff. The back-room was perfectly empty.

By this time it was about five o'clock, so we agreed to keep guard alternately until the following morning, by watching three hours each ; Savrimovitch to take the first watch, Mouravioff the second, I the third, and so on. We decided also to use the back-room which looked towards the Turks as our watch-room. The enemy's advanced post was only two hundred yards off.

We next proposed to make ourselves as comfortable as circumstances would permit. The evening was excessively close. We divested ourselves of our belts and accoutrements, and unbuttoned our tunics; indeed, the Russians, who seemed to feel the heat more than I did, tore open the front of their shirts as well. I observed that each of them wore a gold locket round his neck. Thinking that they were love tokens, I made some chaffing remark about them, but Savrimovitch gravely informed me that I was mistaken, and handed me his locket, which contained a beautifully executed picture of the Madonna. Mouravioff, who was an avowed sceptic in matters of religion, flippantly remarked that he only wore his charm to oblige a lady relative, who believed that it would render him invulnerable to Turkish bullets.

For some time Mouravioff and I chatted pleasantly about various topics. Suddenly an exclamation from the watch-room startled us.

"Hulloh, Savrimovitch! Do you see anything?" cried Mouravioff.

"No," replied the other, "but I can hear the Turks. Listen a moment, they are singing." We kept silence for a minute or two, and heard our enemies indulging in a wild but monotonous chant, or rather howling, the burden of which seemed to be—

"Ya! Allah! Hoo Allah!"

We thought at first that this might presage an attack, and seized our weapons ; but as time went on, and they made no signs of advancing, we became reassured, and prepared and ate our evening meal. At eight o'clock Mouravioff mounted guard in place of Savrimovitch. The moon was now shedding a flood of silvery light upon our cottage, the adjacent forests, the hills beyond ; the sky was studded with innumerable stars, which shone and twinkled with a brilliancy far exceeding anything seen in the heavier atmosphere of England.   From a tree close by a night-bird was filling the air with liquid notes of great sweetness and purity ; and while two armies were encamped within a mile of us, only waiting for an opportunity to rush at one another, the whole scene around seemed to breathe nothing but peace.

My thoughts wandered thousands of miles away—first to my parents and brothers and sister in Calcutta, and then away to the beautiful Bulgarian, who had captivated my heart at Semendria, and whose presence seemed to haunt me even in the camp.   Once the thought presented itself to me that I might never see them again, but it was immediately and ignominiously expelled, and replaced by a bright vision of their delight when they should hear of my extraordinary achievements as medical Field Marshal, and see the long lists of illustrious personages, from emperors down to mere generals, who had been or were about to be benefited by my skilfully wielded scalpel.

Savrimovitch was sitting near the fire, with his face

buried in his hands, and was apparently lost in a gloomy reverie, "A ducat for your dreams, my boy," said I, laying my hand on his shoulder. "They seem to be dismal."

"They are not very lively," he replied, raising his handsome face, which wore an unusually sad expression. "I have somehow a presentiment that I shall never return from this war. I had a strange dream the other night, which I cannot forget!"

"Pooh," said I, as cheerily as I could, "podophyllin for presentiments! Digestible food for dreams! Colonel Philipovitch's champagne and camping out have disagreed with you. Nothing is more inducive to gloomy forebodings than pork and *pâté de foie gras.* Tell me your horrible dream, and I will try and interpret it for you."

"Thank you," replied he, quietly, "I had rather not speak about it, but," and here he gave a slight shudder, "I believe I had my warning."

"Well, well," said I, "let's change the subject. Suppose we talk about love."

"You will think me a doleful subject, M. Wright," replied he, forcing a smile, "but even love is a painful subject to me."

"How's that?" asked I, with a sympathetic frown; "have the fair but fickle angels treated you badly?"

"No, no," said he, laughing slightly. "On the contrary, I have received nothing but kindness at their hands, and I am entirely devoted to their service."

"You perplex me," said I. "How then can it be painful to you to talk of love?"

"Because I happen to be desperately, but hopelessly, attached to a lady who can never return my affection."

"My dear M. Savrimovitch," said I, quickly, "I am a month or two older than you, and have seen much, very much, of the ways of the world. Permit me, therefore, to tell you that there need be no such thing as hopeless love in this world. Have you ever made any proposal to your lady-love?"

"No," replied he.

"Then," said I, "I have great hopes for you. The very next time you meet the lady, make her a declaration of love; never mind if your first attempt is unsuccessful. The poet wrote the beautiful lines—

> "'If at first you don't succeed,
> Try, try, try again;

chiefly, I believe, for the encouragement of desponding lovers. I don't believe there ever was a maiden who could refuse twenty successive matrimonial proposals from the same pertinacious suitor."

"My dear M. Wright," said he, "you don't know what you are talking about! The lady in question is a Russian Grand Duchess, and since I last had the honour of seeing her she has been married."

"Phew!" whistled I, in amazement, "a Grand Duchess, and married! That does make a difference. I am afraid your case really is hopeless," and I shook

9

my head despondently, "unless you like to wait until
Her Imperial Highness is a widow. But how, in the
name of goodness, came you to fall in love with a
Grand Duchess ? "

" It happened in this wise," said he. " The Czar
annually gives a ball in the Winter Palace to the
officers of the Guard, when the lady members of the
Imperial family honour the officers by dancing with
some of them. Russian Court etiquette forbids any
officer to ask a Grand Duchess to dance with him, so
the Imperial lady indicates to the Lord Chamberlain
the officer she chooses for her partner, and he straightway introduces the lucky guardsman. Well, on two
occasions I had the supreme felicity, or rather the
terrible misfortune, of dancing with the same princess,
with the result that I have been hopelessly and despairingly in love with her ever since."

At this juncture we heard a peculiar whining noise
close outside, accompanied by a scratching at the
door.

We all sprang to our feet at once. Mouravioff and
Savrimovitch seized their revolvers, and I whipped my
trusty cutlass out of its sheath.

" Deuced odd sound that ! " said I, in some alarm.
" What on earth can it be ? "

" I'll soon see," said Savrimovitch, and striding to
the door he quickly swung it open. Lo, there was
nothing to be seen ! But we heard a sound as if
something or somebody were scuttling away in a great

hurry. Mouravioff stepped outside and looked around. All was as still as death. "There's *diablerie* in this," said Savrimovitch, looking slightly scared, and probably thinking of his presentiments; and I must confess that I, too, felt half-inclined to ascribe the sounds to something supernatural.

"*Diablerie,* pooh! A dog or a donkey more likely; at any rate, it doesn't matter to us what it is, so long as it is not a Turk," said the matter-of-fact Mouravioff.

"Let's leave the door slightly open," said I, "and we'll watch for it, whatever it is; Savrimovitch and I on this side, and you through the window on the opposite side of the cottage."

They agreed to this, and we commenced our watch, not without a good deal of dread and some curiosity on my part, for it occurred to me that the late occupants of the place might have been murdered by Bashi-Bazouks, and that their shades were hovering around us. We listened for some minutes in breathless silence for the slightest sound. The night-bird had stopped his song, and we could hear nothing but the sighing of the wind in the forest leaves. Suddenly Mouravioff gave a loud laugh, and exclaimed,—

"*Parbleu!* Here comes your devil! Here comes your fiend! Look, Savrimovitch! look, M. Wright! Ah! he's going round to your door—look!"

We put our heads outside the door, and just as we did so a large black dog rounded the corner of the building, and came straight up to the door. As soon as it saw us, however, it scurried away to some distance, and sitting on its haunches set up a most melancholy howling.

Mouravioff and I looked at one another, and burst out laughing at this unromantic elucidation of the mystery.   To my surprise, however, I noticed that Savrimovitch was pale and agitated.

" How peculiarly that dog howls ! " said he, with a shiver.   " Does it not seem to you that there is something weird and unnatural in the sound ? "

" Why, Savrimovitch," said Mouravioff, " what nonsense is this ?   You are as pale as a ghost, and shaking like an aspen.   Are you ill ? "

" No, it's nothing, thanks ; a little dizziness, no more.   There, I'm all right now," said he, drawing himself up to his full height, " and fit for anything. You may laugh if you like, but I tell you candidly I would rather have seen twenty Turks just then than that dog.   Whenever a misfortune is about to befall our family, a hound like that makes its appearance, and howls as that one is doing." Savrimovitch's explanation made a considerable impression upon me, but Mouravioff laughed aloud.

" Stuff and nonsense," said he, " that dog's no demon. I am surprised that a *stout* soldier should be (I trust I sha'n't offend you) so absurdly superstitious.   Here, M. Wright, kindly pass the spirits round, and let us have a glass apiece.   Let me pour you out a bumper, Savrimovitch   you're in a fanciful mood to-night, and need a

tonic; low spirits require a pick-me-up! We'll keep our
spirits up by pouring spirits down!"

The usually cynical Mouravioff was in high spirits this
evening, and displayed an amount of kindliness and good-
humour for which I had not given him credit. At eleven
o'clock I mounted guard, and my two friends rolled
themselves up in their overcoats and went to sleep.

Nothing happened during my three hours' watch. I
had great difficulty in keeping myself awake, and was
very glad when it was time to rouse Savrimovitch and
relegate my duties to him. Then I threw myself on to
the heap of grain and almost immediately fell asleep.
I had perhaps been asleep for an hour, when a violent
blow on the side and a loud scuffling noise awoke me.
Starting up, I beheld a man struggling desperately with
Savrimovitch, who held him fast by the throat.

The Russian was a powerful young man, but no match
for his opponent, who seemed possessed of Herculean
strength, and whose uniform and swarthy complexion
proclaimed him a Turk. Before we could rush to our
friend's assistance the combatants fell with a crash to the
ground, the intruder uppermost, and brandishing a formidable Circassian knife in his hand. He had no time
to use it, however, for Mouravioff struck him a terrible
blow on the head with his clubbed rifle, and he rolled
over senseless. To our unspeakable relief Savrimovitch rose to his feet uninjured, vowing that he had
tripped over some inequality on the floor. After this
sudden and unexpected attack we all kept on the alert

with our weapons in our hands for some time, but the
Turks in the opposite woods showed no signs of moving,
and the stillness of the night was unbroken.   In answer
to our eager queries, Savrimovitch said that he had kept a
sharp look-out on the Turkish side, and that our prisoner
must have skirted the clearing and approached the hut
from behind, and that when they met the Turk seemed
as much surprised as he had been.   This explanation
reassured us, and led us to the conclusion that the Turk
had been in the habit of helping himself to the maize
that lay in the hut.   Having satisfied myself that we were
not going to be attacked just then, I left the two
Russians to watch and prepare breakfast, and proceeded
with feelings of the liveliest enthusiasm to examine the
injuries of our captive.   He was still comatose, and his
breathing was stertorous.   I discovered, with sensations
of sympathy and satisfaction, that he had sustained a
depressed fracture of the skull, and that an immediate
operation was necessary.   I will not harrow the feelings of
my non-professional readers by describing the measures
I adopted, but will content myself with saying that I
succeeded, not without considerable difficulty, in elevating
the depressed piece of bone.   The condition was at once
greatly improved.

" Bravo, doctor ! " exclaimed Mouravioff, " but what
are you going to do now ? " (I had produced my beloved
amputating case and a pair of bullet forceps.)   " You are .
surely not going to cut off his head ?"

To this ridiculous question I replied with the gravity

of tone a medical man should always adopt when speaking to a layman on professional subjects, that I could see no necessity for removing his head, and that I was merely about to institute a search for old gun-shot wounds, as it was quite possible that my patient might have a bullet in him which required extraction.

"I should have thought, doctor," said Savrimovitch (I noticed with much gratification that they called me doctor now), "that he struggled much too vigorously for that."

" My dear Savrimovitch," replied I, ripping up the prisoner's garments and exploring his limbs, "fear and excitement often inspire the weakest and the completely disabled with remarkable strength. We have a saying in England which is doubtless intended to be illustrative of this fact, but which, of course, is not to be interpreted literally, that King Charles I. walked and talked half an hour after his head was cut off; and I myself have seen fowls leap into the air and run about for some seconds after decapitation."

The sceptical Mouravioff laughed loudly, and even the courteous Savrimovitch looked incredulous, but I was far too much interested in the work I had in hand to take any notice of either of them.

To my disappointment I found no old bullet wound on the prisoner, but my desire to confer further surgical blessings on our barbarian captive was not altogether thwarted. I perceived that he had a small epitheliomatous ulcer on the lower lip. I decided there and then on its removal, and explaining the malignant nature of the lesion to the Russians, cut away the affected part, without the slightest objection from my patient. Perhaps I ought to add that he remained insensible the whole time, but if he had been conscious, no reasonable person could suppose but that he would have submitted cheerfully—nay, gladly—to an operation fraught with such advantage to himself. I then dressed his lip, and putting my head out of the window, sniffed up the fresh morning air, and gave myself up to the complacent mental gratification which is the proper reward of every good deed. In very truth, I had heaped coals of fire on my adversary's head!

It was now nearly four o'clock; the grey dawn was giving place to the brighter light of day, and a crimson flush suffused the eastern sky. I watched the changing of the tints and brightening of the light with much pleasure, when suddenly the flash of musketry sparkled forth from the opposite trees, and I had just time to withdraw my head, when a bullet whistled through the window and knocked a large piece of dry mud and plaster from the wall of the apartment. Half-a-dozen Turks issued from the wood and advanced towards us at a run, headed by an officer, who held a revolver in one hand and brandished a gleaming sabre in the other. The whole thing was so sudden that I was thoroughly scared; however, I thrust the muzzle of my rifle through the window, and taking a hurried aim at the leader of the party, pulled the trigger. The report of my piece was followed

"HALF-A-DOZEN TURKS, WITH AN OFFICER AT THEIR HEAD RUSHED OUT AT US."

To face p. 144.]

immediately by the loud bang-bang ! of the rifles of my friends, who had rushed outside at the first alarm. When the smoke cleared away, the Turkish officer, evidently severely wounded, was being raised from the ground by a couple of his men, and the others were retreating to the forest at the double. Our triumph was very short-lived. Bugles rang out and shouts resounded from various parts of the forest, showing that the other Turkish outposts and pickets had taken the alarm, and that more men were hastening to attack us.

"M. Alfred, M. Wright!" shouted Mouravioff and Savrimovitch, entering the cottage, "come away, come away; we've no time to lose! In two minutes the place will be surrounded!" I was reluctant to leave my patient, who still lay helpless on the ground, though he was now showing signs of returning animation (I had quite discarded the notion of standing a six months' siege in the cottage); but the enemy now reopened fire on us from the wood, and the bullets whistled about the place so unpleasantly that I was glad to hurry away. By keeping the little building between ourselves and the enemy we succeeded in getting a good way off before we were discovered. But presently a loud shout proclaimed to us that we had been seen, and that we should have to run the gauntlet. We hurried up the hill-side, under a smart rifle fire, towards the Servian camp, and fortunately reached the trench uninjured when we met a body of Servian soldiers hastening downwards, headed by fat Colonel Philipovitch, who was in a very

excited state and much out of breath. He saw us, and
gave a loud halloo of surprise and delight.

"Or—or, dear frents! dear frents! I thought you
was killed, and all dead; now I am glad ever so much
more—ha! ha!" exclaimed he, and flinging down his
drawn sabre he embraced all three of us, one after the
other, most vigorously, sobbing and laughing alternately.
When he became a little calmer he told us that he had
not slept a wink all night, and that at the sound of the
firing he took it for granted that we had been surprised
and killed, and was coming down to recover our bodies
and avenge our deaths. Then stepping back a pace or
two, he scanned us from head to foot, and eagerly asked
if any of us had been hurt. We assured him that we
were all right, on the strength of which he gave each of
us another suffocating hug, and then marched back with
us to his quarters. On the way we related our adventures, which, simple as they were, filled him with
astonishment and admiration. When Savrimovitch—who,
being the best linguist amongst us, acted as our spokes-
man—told him of the strange scratching noise heard
outside the hut and of the mysterious dog, his fat face
turned pale, and his stubbly hair stood on end with
superstitious awe. When he heard of the capture of
our prisoner, he broke forth into a torrent of sympathetic
and enthusiastic braves and bravissimos! He was
much disgusted with my attempt to set the wounded
Turk to rights again, and rolling his eyes about in a
manner that was frightful to behold, drew his hand

significantly across his throat, as much as to say that I
should have done much better if I had made an end of
him (the prisoner) instead.

On our arrival at the colonel's tent we found a really
sumptuous breakfast spread, which we attacked with keen
relish, and immediately after the meal we prepared to
start for Deligrad again.   Our kind entertainer was most
anxious that we should prolong our stay with him, but
this, we explained to him, was quite impossible, and
taking a really affecting leave of this warm-hearted
soul, we got·into our cart and trundled off to our own
camp.

CHAPTER XV.

W E reached the Medvedovski camp the same afternoon, and found it in an unwonted state of excitement. A gorgeous silken banner, the handiwork of some Russian ladies sympathetic with the Servian cause, and which had been consecrated by the Metropolitan of Moscow, had just arrived, and General Tchernaieff was coming to present it formally to the brigade.

The whole brigade was under arms, and we had hardly time to fall into our battalion. The troops were marched to a large open space a few hundred yards to the right of the camp, and formed into an immense hollow square. General Tchernaieff then rode up, surrounded by his staff, and dismounting, entered the square, where he was received by Colonel Medvedovski, some of the other officers of the brigade, and three priests. Amongst the general's staff a stout, sleek-looking young man was pointed out to me as the Roumanian Prince, Ghika, and I also saw for the first time that well-known English or rather Scottish soldier of fortune, Colonel McIvor. One of the priests opened the proceedings with a long prayer, during which the soldiers crossed themselves incessantly. Holy water was then sprinkled on the banner, and General Tchernaieff, taking it from the priests, made a speech to the brigade, and presented it to Colonel Medvedovski, who in turn handed it to one of his officers. Then the whole brigade was marched in single file past the priest, beside whom was a small altar with a cross on it, and each man as he passed was touched on the lips and forehead with a spray of hyssop dipped in holy water.

This ceremony lasted an immense time, and the priest's arms must have fairly ached by the time it was over. I witnessed these proceedings with the greatest interest and enthusiasm. Here was a magnificent opportunity of distinguishing myself. I resolved on the spot to ask for the proud privilege of carrying the banner the first time we went into action ! Thousands of men would go into battle, but only one could be the standard-bearer at a time.

" This," thought I, " will distinguish me above my fellows, and maintain my reputation as a brave Englishman ! "

When the ceremony was over, I mentioned my scheme to Savrimovitch. He heartily approved of it, so the next morning I went to the colonel for the purpose of preferring my request to him.

" Well, sir," said he on seeing me, " what can I do for you ? "

" I have come, sir," replied I, " to ask if you will let me carry the standard that was presented to us yesterday into action the first time we are engaged."

The colonel looked very pleased, but for a moment

said nothing; then he observed that if I would call again the next day at noon he would give me an answer. Delays of any description are very disagreeable to me, so I felt slightly disappointed at the reply, still I saluted with a good grace and went away.

On the following day I presented myself at the appointed hour, and with my heart full of hope and expectation. The colonel received me most graciously, and beside him were Count Réné and Prince Obolenski, both of whom shook hands with me with kind cordiality.

" Well, sir," said the Brigadier, "your request has pleased us very much ; it shows us that you are actuated by a loyal and worthy spirit. Nevertheless, this brigade is, *par excellence,* the Russian brigade, therefore we think it better that a Russian should carry the colours."

I suppose my face displayed the disappointment I felt, for the colonel continued—

" I am very sorry to refuse your request, but never fear, you will soon have plenty of opportunities of showing what stuff you are made of ! "

I walked back dolefully enough, and confided my trouble to Savrimovitch, who seemed, however, to be brooding over some trouble of his own, and was less sympathetic than usual.

The heat that afternoon was intense, and Savrimovitch, Mouravioff, and I were silently smoking under the shelter of our hut, when a bullet whistled between us, and passed out through the leafy wall behind. We started to our feet and rushed outside.

A number of soldiers were standing or sitting about engaged in cleaning their rifles, cooking, etc. Mouravioff demanded furiously who had fired the shot.

A heavy, stupid-looking fellow was pointed out as the culprit, whereupon our friend strode up to him, and seizing him by the collar, asked him sternly what he meant by discharging a loaded rifle in camp. The soldier sulkily answered that he had only fired his piece in the air, and did not know there was any harm in that, whereupon the rough-and-ready Mouravioff replied—

"Idiot ! Don't you know that when you send a bullet into the air it is likely to come down again, like this ? " and striking him on the head with his clenched fist, knocked him over.

This severe treatment caused some murmuring amongst the soldiers, who were already beginning to tire of Russian discipline. A sinister rumour that many Russian officers had been treacherously slain in battle by some of their own men, whose ill-will they had incurred, was current in camp, and it was undoubtedly true that Russian officers frequently treated the Servians with great harshness, but considering the rawness and inaptitude of the material they had to deal with, and the absolute necessity of enforcing discipline, I do not think that the kicks and cuffs I often saw them bestow on their men were unmerited.

Again, although the unwarlike Serbs murmured at being dragooned into discipline, they seemed very soon to regain their equanimity. They are naturally too good-natured and easy-going a race to be vindictive, and therefore I believe that the heavy losses among the Russians were due to their reckless valour and not to Servian treachery. Nevertheless, many Russians I met firmly believed this rumour, in spite of the indignant denial of it given by the Servians.

As the days passed by, I noticed with pain that my friend Savrimóvitch became more and more reserved and melancholy, and that every now and then he would fly on the slightest provocation, or even without any at all, into the most ungovernable fury. On one occasion he took offence at something Count Tiesenhausen said to him, and calling him a German coward, drew his revolver, and would certainly have shot him if I had not disarmed him.

Another time he came up to me and asked me to give him enough opium to make away with himself. On these occasions he looked and behaved like a madman. He said that he was tired of life, and wished to die. Of course I refused his request. For a minute or two he pressed me earnestly, nay, coaxingly, to give him the opium, and when I persisted in my refusal he laid his hand on his sword, and with flushed face and flashing eyes told me he would compel me to give him what he wanted. Up to this time I had tried to laugh him out of the idea, but his furious and menacing attitude made me serious.

"My dear friend," said I, looking him steadily in the face, "you will not get a grain of opium from me. If you wish to die, you will soon have abundant opportunities of satisfying your desire when we go into action. If you were to poison yourself now, it might be said that you were afraid to face the Turks. Is it not far better to fall like a brave soldier than to die of poison like a rat?"

At the end of my speech the wild glare left Savrimovitch's eyes and the crimson flush died out of his cheeks. He threw down his sword, and embracing me called me his English brother, and begged me to forgive his frenzied petulance, then passing his hand across his forehead he said, "When these whirlwinds of fury seize my mind, I feel like a tiger or a madman, and lose all self-control. Two or three years ago I received this sabre wound," and he showed me a scar on the side of his head concealed by his hair, "and I have never been the same since. Lately, though, I have become more irritable and excitable than ever, and I wish, like a dear good fellow, you would look after me. You have a strange influence over me, and may be the means of preventing me from doing some irreparable mischief."

Then we kissed after the Russian fashion, vowed eternal friendship, and agreed henceforth to call one another by our Christian names of Alfred and Alexis.

Alexis' favourite topic of conversation was India. He was never tired of asking questions about that marvellous country, or hearing stories of encounters with tigers, elephants, and wild boars in the jungles; of adventures with crocodiles and venomous snakes,

10

and fights with pirates by land and sea, of which I had learned any number from my Anglo-Indian uncles and aunts.

My tales fired his imagination to such a degree that he resolved to go for a tour in India after the war was over, and asked me to accompany him, which I agreed to do. I now noticed, with gratification, an improvement in my friend's mental condition. Both his fits of depression and his outbreaks of temper became less intense and less frequent. This satisfactory result was partly due to the fact that I contrived in various ways to divert his attention from himself, and also because he made a real effort to exercise more self-control.

His state of mind was never such as to incapacitate him from attending to his duties ; indeed, everything that he had to do was well and thoroughly done, and it was only during his idle moments, and when he was interfered with, that he behaved strangely. Still, his conduct was at times very unaccountable, sufficiently so to justify the belief that his reason was within a measurable distance of becoming permanently impaired.

He attributed his condition to the sabre wound he had received on his head, and that had, in all probability, a great deal to do with it. *Apropos* of this wound, I asked him one day how he received it, and the following was his account :—

"I went out as a volunteer with General Kaufmann's army during the late campaign against the Turcomans.

One bitterly cold winter's day, when the plains were thickly covered with snow, I accompanied a detachment of fifty Cossacks on a reconnoitring expedition. As we were returning, snow began to fall heavily, and the consequence was we came unawares upon a large body of the enemy. They were all of them mounted and were headed by a chief on a magnificent black horse. As soon as they saw us, they raised a fierce shout and dashed at us at a gallop. So swift was their approach that my men had just time to give them a volley from their carbines and to level their lances, when they swept upon us like a whirlwind, and surrounded us on all sides, cutting, thrusting, and hewing at us with the fury of demons. Though my men were outnumbered, ten to one, they fought with desperate valour, for they knew that no quarter would be given them. As if by mutual consent, the chief on the black horse and I singled each other out, but the press was so great that after we had exchanged a cut or two we were separated. Twice we succeeded in cutting our way through the Turcoman host, only to find ourselves surrounded again, and our condition began to look hopeless indeed. Numbers of the enemy, it is true, had fallen, but we had also lost heavily, and could ill afford to do so. My sword arm became so tired that I could hardly raise it, and all my men were suffering either from wounds or exhaustion. Still we fought on, hoping against hope, that the discharge of our carbines might be heard from our camp and assistance be sent to us. Whilst I was defending myself against another man, the Turcoman chief attacked me again, and aimed a terrible cut at my head. I saw it coming, and tried to parry it, but ineffectually. My guard was beaten down, and the blow descended on me, inflicting the wound you see, and knocking me from my saddle. The chief was about to finish me off with another stroke, when one of my men ran him through the body with his lance. I recollect nothing more about the affair, except that I found myself in our camp hospital the next day, with my head aching terribly, and covered with dressings and bandages; our firing, it seems, had been heard, and a rescue sent, but only just in time, for my little band had been reduced to fifteen men, not one of whom was unwounded."

Some days after this conversation we got leave to go to Paratchin. My friend was very fond of riding, and tried hard to borrow a couple of horses for the occasion. However, he was unsuccessful, and was grievously disappointed thereat. I expressed much sympathy with him, but really felt much relieved, for I was by no means a good horseman. However, we managed to borrow a dingy-looking, but comfortable open carriage, which actually boasted of good springs, and left the camp in it one morning, amidst the envious remarks of our brother officers and the admiring criticisms of the men. When we were about four miles from Paratchin, we were overtaken by three officers

on horseback, one of whom proved to be the young
man who bore so striking a resemblance to Marie!
He looked into our carriage as he passed, and as
our eyes met he blushed to his temples, and hurriedly
returning our salutation, turned his face away, and
putting spurs to his horse galloped off.

"What a shy-looking young fellow that is!" said
Savrimovitch. "He looks more like a girl than a man,
doesn't he? Still he rides well."

"I've seen him before somewhere," said I.

"Do you know anything about him?"

"Nothing," was the reply.

On arriving at Paratchin, we told the driver to go to
the best hotel, and he took us to one called the Kneas
Serbski (Servian Prince.)

We went into the coffee-room, which was crowded with
Servian soldiers and officers, feeding and smoking, and
ordered a substantial dinner. Whilst we were waiting
for it to be served, who should I see, extended on a
bench by the wall, but my distinguished Belgrade
acquaintance, Colonel Bragg, of dog-slaying and swearing celebrity!

Although I was not one of that hero's admirers, I
was concerned to see that he looked pale and miserable,
and leaving my seat for a moment, I went up to the
colonel, and saluting him, expressed a hope that he was
well.

"Who the——are you? Ah, I know! The little doctor
who came to see me in a pair of d——d stupid india-

rubber boots ; I hope you are better than I am.   I'm
d——d bad I can tell you ! "

"What is the matter, sir ? " said I.   " Perhaps I can
do something for you ? "

" I don't know what's the matter, doctor," said he,
" but I've been d——d ill this last ten days.   Rheuma-
tism, gout, or some kind of fever or another.   It was
a confounded shame to send me to the front; I'm not
fit for it."

" Let's look at your tongue," said I.

" No, I sha'n't," said he, "what good will that do? All
I want is to keep quiet."   Then raising himself on his
elbow, and drawing me closer to him, he said in a
whisper, " I say, doctor, couldn't you give me a certificate
to the effect that I am too ill to go to the front? I'm
d——d fond of fighting," here he gave a sickly smile,
" but I'm not fit to go.   These mulligrubs, you know,
are the very devil; they are playing old Harry with me."
Before I could reply a loud and wrathful exclamation
from Savrimovitch startled me.   Turning round I saw
him, his face crimson with fury, seize a wine bottle by
the neck and fling it with all his force at the head of
one of the waiters.   The bottle struck the man on the
back of the head and smashed into a thousand pieces,
deluging him with its contents, and sending a shower
of wine and pieces of glass over several of the
tables.

Immediately the whole place became a pandemonium.
Every one sprang to his feet, tables were overturned, and

plates and dishes fell clattering and smashing on to the floor. Swords leaped from their scabbards, and the air resounded with oaths and imprecations, and in place of a party of merry fellows enjoying their dinners, one could see nothing but angry faces and bristling weapons and general confusion.

In the middle of all this turmoil stood Savrimovitch, sword in hand, defying the tempest he had raised with angry, scornful contempt and jibing temper.

Though I inwardly cursed his hasty temper, it was impossible for me to leave him in this pickle, so quickly drawing my cutlass I placed myself alongside of him, and looked terrific things at the wrathful mob that surrounded us.

For about a second we faced one another ; then, as if with one accord, they rushed at us. I was overwhelmed with a storm of blows, knocked down, and my sword forced out of my hand. I recollect struggling desperately to get up and receiving another blow on the head. After that a faint, giddy feeling came over me, and I lost consciousness. When I came to, it was to find myself in a darkened room, with a very vague idea of what had taken place or of where I was. In the middle of my speculations on these two points, I was disturbed by the flash of a light and the sound of footsteps entering the room, and looking up saw the young Bulgarian officer who so much reminded me of Marie, accompanied by Doctor Yermaylaff Giggleivitch.

A half-muttered exclamation from me brought the

young officer to my bedside, with clasped hands and a look of the most anxious interest in his face.

"I am so glad, sir," said he, "to find you better. I trust that you are not suffering much pain."

Convinced that this young man was no other than Marie, I foolishly said—

"I am ever so much better already, and if you will only come and see me every day, Marie, I shall soon be well again."

But I had not finished the sentence before I saw the mistake I had made. The young officer drew himself up stiffly, and said with a frown—

"My name, sir, is Milosch Darvorin;" and then turning to the doctor, added, "I thought that he was better, but he is still delirious. Had we not better leave him?"

Agonized at the thought of having offended one to please whom I would have given worlds, I exclaimed—

"Yes, I am delirious; I don't know what I am saying. I assure you, sir, that I am a miserable fool, who having but little sense to begin with has now lost that little. I trust, therefore" (here I cast an imploring glance at the young officer), "that you will not take offence at anything I may have said." At this pathetic appeal both the doctor and the young officer laughed; the former, however, suddenly checking his merriment, came to the side of the bed and said drily—

"I quite agree with you, sir, as to your having no sense, and unless you keep perfectly quiet you'll have no life either. Not another word, sir; your recovery and my reputation, which I have staked upon it, depend on your having complete rest and keeping silence." With these words Dr. Giggleivitch and his companion left the room, and I was again alone and in darkness.

CHAPTER XVI.

M Y mind was still in a considerable muddle, and when I was left to myself I pondered hazily over what Marie or rather Milosch Darvorin and that confounded Dr. Giggleivitch had said to me, when all at once I began to wonder what had become of Savrimovitch. When I last saw him, he was fighting desperately by my side, and after that my recollection failed me.

I was afraid he might be dead, and felt terribly uneasy and anxious about him. Luckily, however, for my peace of mind, Dr. Giggleivitch came into my room again, and I seized the opportunity and asked him about my friend.

" I told you not to talk just now, sir," said he, sternly, and without answering my question.

" Yes, I know you did, doctor, but I must know; for Heaven's sake tell me what has become of Alexis Savrimovitch, and I promise I won't talk any more."

" He's alive, and doing very well; drink this ; " and he gave me a filthy draught of some sort, and walked out of the room again.

My mind was relieved, and when I awoke next

morning I felt refreshed and much better. But I had received such a mauling that I could not leave my bed for a week. I had three nasty scalp wounds and a sabre cut across my forehead, which I am afraid will permanently mar my beauty. I was not allowed to see Savrimovitch for some while, but one day he stalked into my room, looking very pale and handsome, and with his left arm in a sling. I was sitting up in bed, a still more dilapidated-looking object.

" My dear Alfred," said he, in a voice full of emotion, " can you forgive me for having brought all this trouble upon you? "

" My dear boy," said I, quite distressed to see him so moved, "you have nothing to reproach yourself with. The Servians are the most quarrelsome and cantankerous set of fellows I ever came across."

" No, it was my fault entirely," said he. " I ought not to have got into such a rage with the waiter, but I had called on the fellow twenty times to serve us, and he paid no attention, and went on attending to everybody else first—at least, so it seemed to me. Then I got angry, and spoke sharply to him, and he had the audacity to tell me I must wait my turn! Confound the fellow's impudence! , I feel warm when I think of it ;" and the peppery Alexis stamped his foot and got into quite a passion at the recollection of it.

" Well," said I, " and what happened then ? "

" Why, I lost my temper, and threw a bottle of wine at him, which smashed into a thousand pieces, and flew

all over the Servians, who were all on the grin, and made
them laugh the wrong side of their mouths."

"And then ? "

"Then they made a great show of jumping to their
feet and drawing their swords, so I called them a lot of
cowardly Turkish slaves, and told them to come on if
they dared. And the rest you know——"

"But what happened after I was cut down ? "

"Cut down ! You weren't cut down at all ; you were
knocked down with a chair, and I shared the same
ignominious fate ; the same blackguard did for us both.
He smashed my sword blade into twenty pieces, and
broke my arm with the same disgusting weapon. I wish
I had the chair-wielding scoundrel here, and my sword
at his throat, I'd teach him a lesson ! "

The entry of a servant with our dinner put an agreeable end to the conversation. I was not sorry, for
Savrimovitch was getting so excited that I almost feared
another outbreak on his part.

After this we were allowed to share the same room,
and both made rapid strides towards recovery. Every
now and then we received a visit from some of our
brother officers at the camp, and one day the Count
Réné came to see us.

"Ah, young fire-eaters ! " he said, after shaking hands
with us, " this sort of thing won't do at all ; you will be
giving the brigade quite a bad name. The colonel was
very vexed when he heard of your little escapade here.
Tell me all about it."

When the count heard our story, he twirled his little shadowy yellow moustache, and said that he did not think we were altogether to blame, " only," he added, " I really do think that an Englishman and a Russian ought to have given a better account of those Servians. By the way, M. Wright," he went on to say, " I have a newspaper here which contains an extract which may probably interest you ; " and with his eyes twinkling with merriment he took from his pocket an English newspaper and handed it to me. It was a copy of the *Daily Courier*, in which was the following paragraph :—

" FIENDISH SERVIAN ATROCITY.—It is my painful duty to have to record the following fiendish outrage which was perpetrated by a party of Servian marauders on a wounded Turkish soldier. I can vouch for the truth of the incident. On the — inst. the Turkish advanced posts near Jubovac discovered that a cottage close to their position was in the hands of the Servians. Captain Hussein Avni, and half a company of the — battalion, instantly attacked and drove out the enemy, not, however, without loss, for the gallant captain was severely wounded in the leg. On entering the cottage, the soldiers found the senseless body of one of their comrades stretched on the floor. The poor fellow was most shockingly mutilated. Not content with slicing off his upper lip, the barbarians had committed the atrocity of drilling a hole in his skull. The indignation excited throughout the army by this piece of devilment is extreme, and we hear that Adul Kerim has sent a *parlementaire*, with a strongly-worded remonstrance on the subject to the Servian headquarters."

This atrocious paragraph overwhelmed me with consternation and dismay. I had hoped and expected that my careful treatment of our Turkish captive's wounds would have gained me no little *kudos,* instead of which it was looked upon as a blood-curdling instance of Bashi-Bazoukism, and I was described as a diabolical monster.

The paper fell from my hands, and I gazed alternately at the count and Alexis in utter bewilderment. My friends did not sympathise with me. On the contrary, they burst into an uncontrollable fit of laughter, which completed my discomfiture and mortification.

"Confound it all! What are you laughing at?" cried I, beside myself with rage. My anger increased their merriment, and they laughed until the tears ran down their cheeks. I felt a strong inclination to quarrel with them for their ill-timed hilarity, but I reflected in time that laughter is a physiological process, which as often as not takes place quite independent of the will. Something tickles that part of the nervous organisation which corresponds with the fancy, and a peculiar stimulus is reflected to the diaphragm, and causes it to move spasmodically, in such a way that the air is jerked from the larynx with an asinine ha! ha! hee! hee! hau! hau! sound. The thought that I had set these doughty Russian warriors braying like a couple of asses more than atoned for the want of sympathy they had shown me. I folded my arms, and awaited their return to gravity with the most perfect equanimity. Of course they were profuse in their apologies, which, however, I assured them were quite unnecessary, for their laughter had afforded me the greatest possible amusement.

Before he went, Count Réné informed us that he had some grand news.

"What is it?" we asked.

"Next week the brigade is to join Horvatovitch's army. That means that we shall have some fighting directly, for Horvatovitch is a fighting fellow. What do you say to that, boys?"

At this delightful piece of intelligence we both gave a loud hurrah. Alexis fell on the count's neck and kissed him, and I executed a warlike and spirited *pas seul* on the floor of the ward.

Our enthusiasm greatly pleased the count, and he bade us adieu with a sweet smile on his weather-beaten countenance.

CHAPTER XVII.

THE count's invigorating news, combined with Dr. Giggleivitch's skilful treatment and disagreeable prescriptions, soon completed my restoration to health, so that within a week of the visit of the former we were back again at Deligrad.

The day after our return our brigade received orders to march to Jubovac, when we occupied the ground that Colonel Philipovitch's men had held, and we were consequently in full view of that never-to-be-forgotten cottage of hateful memory. For the first few days at Jubovac the weather was terribly bad. The sun was invisible, and the rain came down in torrents, and mud and slush prevailed everywhere. Sometimes on waking in the morning, I found myself half smothered in a pool of water which had collected in the depression made by my weight in the soft soil. To add to my discomfort, Savrimovitch, who up to this time had shared his waterproof with me, was appointed adjutant to the brigade, and now seldom slept in our part of the camp. It is not very surprising, therefore, that I began to suffer from ague. Several of the Russians, however, regarded my seediness as a proof of their theory that Englishmen might be

A BULGARIAN VOLUNTEER.

To face p. 168.]

brave, but had no stamina, and one of them had the assurance to tell me so to my face. I determined, if possible, to cure myself straight away, and with that object in view I stirred a whole teaspoonful of quinine into a wineglass full of Raki, and tossed the mixture off. Heavens! what a bitter draught it was, and what a head-ache it gave me! However, it answered its purpose, and cured me for the time being of ague.

Besides the wet, we had every now and then to put up with very short commons in the way of provisions, due, I suppose, to some temporary breakdown in the Commissariat Department. More than once the only dinner I got during the day was a piece of bread and a roasted onion, supplemented with a dessert of acorns and wild honey, luxuries with which the oak forest surrounding us abounded. As if to tantalize us, the peasants used to drive their herds of swine into these forests, where the herbage and fallen berries supplied them with plenty of fattening food.

For the protection of these precious pigs Colonel Horvatovitch had issued the most stringent regulations. They were private property—so went his decree—and the troops were forbidden to touch them, under the severest pains and penalties. In spite of these threats, of which, at the time, I knew nothing, pigs were mysteriously murdered and pork surreptitiously devoured almost every day in some part or other of the camp.

The peasants became clamorous about their slaughtered swine, and Horvatovitch, in a rage, instituted pig-protect-

ing patrols, and vowed that he would hang the first pig-
sticker who fell into his clutches.

One day, when we had been particularly badly off for
food, Savrimovitch, Mouravioff, and I went for a stroll
into the woods. We were all very hungry, and I, at
least, was in blissful ignorance of the commander's pig-
protecting *pronunciamento*. We were sauntering along
quietly under the shade of the trees, when the grunting
of a porker greeted our ears. We exchanged significant
glances, my friends, doubtless, thinking of the regulations,
whilst I smacked my lips in anticipation of a delicious ·
meal of roast pork with crackling. The next moment a
luscious spectacle burst upon our enraptured gaze ! Two
fat pigs, in the very pink of condition for eating, and
with the curliest of tails, trotted into view, and with a
series of happy and contented grunts, commenced
muzzling and guzzling amongst the roots and berries
that lay about them. The prospect of crackling over-
came me ! In the twinkling of an eye I had raised my
rifle to my shoulder, and sent a bullet through the head
of the nearest. I sprang forward with a shout of triumph
to secure my prey, and laughingly called on Alexis and
Mouravioff to assist me, but neither of them stirred.

"Heavens, M. Wright !" said Alexis, "what have
you done ?"

"Have you not heard fire-eating Horvatovitch's pro-
clamation of death to the pig-slayer ?" said Mouravioff.

"Murder !" said I. "You don't mean to say that it
is forbidden to kill pigs ?"

"I should rather think it is," was the reply.

"Well, but what would you have me do?" said I, in an agony. "We surely must not leave that lovely carcase there to waste?"

"Well, no," said my friends, who also cast longing glances at it. "It would be a pity to waste it."

"Wait a bit," said Mouravioff. "I'll tell you what will be the best thing to do. Issue invitations to all the officers you know to a supper party this evening; get as many others in the same hunt with yourself, and you'll find it will end all right. The general won't like to punish a score of officers just on the eve of a battle."

The idea seemed to me a good one, so I agreed to adopt it. Meanwhile we covered the beautiful body with leaves in a most artful manner, so that no one would suspect there was a dead pig there, and on our return to camp we directed the handy Yenko to the spot, and commissioned him to cut up the pig and bring it back piece-meal. The astute mannikin succeeded in doing this without being discovered, and we then issued our invitations. About twenty Russian officers, including Counts Tiesenhausen, Réné, and Baron Kleist accepted, and we made a most excellent supper and spent a most enjoyable evening. The next morning, however, whilst I was performing the usual apology for a toilet, an officer, with a guard of soldiers at his back, came up to the tent, and politely requested me to accompany him to the headquarters. I asked him if he would be good enough to wait while I beautified myself for the occasion. He consented, so I made Yenko give my boots, which had not been off my feet for nearly a week, a good greasing (blacking was an ʼunknown luxury in the camp), and put a respectable-looking piece of pink twine to my eyeglass in place of the original black silk cord which had been reduced by hard wear to a disreputable little chain of knots about eighteen inches in length. Moreover, bad weather and rough usage having caused the shedding of most of my buttons, I deemed it advisable to make my pantaloons secure with some stout string, and then distributed my scanty allowance of water for washing as judiciously as possible over my face and hands. These arrangements completed, I bade a dignified farewell to the friends who crowded around, and signifying my readiness to depart to the officer, drew myself up to my full height and strode off with them, erect and calm.

Close to headquarters we passed a party of soldiers leading away two prisoners, whose hands were pinioned behind their backs.

"Hulloh!" said I to my guide, "what have those fellows been up to?"

"Killing pigs, monsieur," was the reply.

"And what's their punishment to be?" inquired I, wincing slightly.

"I believe they are to be hanged, monsieur," said the officer, blandly; "but I am not sure, or it is possible that they will be shot."

"Confound it all!" exclaimed I, much startled; "you don't really mean that?"

"Yes, monsieur, that is what I have heard," said the officer. "The general is determined to make examples of the next pig-killers he catches, but here we are!"

The headquarters were established in a large barn, which at this moment was thronged with officers, some of whom were seated at a table, and seemed to constitute the court martial, whilst others were merely lookers-on. At the head of the table stood a heavily-bearded man of immense stature, fully six feet six in height. His strongly marked but handsome features were flushed, and his blue eyes glittered with anger as I entered, and I noticed with concern that he utterly ignored my salute.

This indignant giant was General Horvatovitch, the biggest and bravest man in the Servian army, and a very stern disciplinarian.

I saw that I was in a desperate scrape, but I cannot say that I felt very much dismayed; on the contrary, the unique and critical position in which I was placed seemed to offer me an excellent opportunity of distinguishing myself, of which I resolved to take full advantage. For a few moments the conclave of officers maintained a low-voiced conversation amongst themselves, in Servian or Russian, of which I understood nothing, and I availed myself of the interval to prepare for what was coming. In the first place, I arranged myself in an attitude that I thought was dignified, easy, and respectful, and assumed an extremely affable expression of countenance. I contrived also to examine the piece of string, and the button which supported my pantaloons.   I thought they "gave" a little, but to my relief they seemed to be all right.   Then I waited calmly for the general to speak.

"What is your name, sir?" said he at last.

"Your highness," said I (I addressed him as highness partly to display my pleasant humour, and partly out of compliment to his great height), "my name is Alfred Wright."

"You are an Englishman?" quoth he.

"I am proud and happy to say that I am, your highness," said I.

"You are charged, sir, with shooting a pig, the property of Jovan Jovanovitch, and stealing its carcase, whereby you have been guilty of disobedience of orders,— a crime which, in time of war, is punishable by death,— and also of looting.   What have you to say in reply?"

"Your highness——" replied I.

"Why, in the fiend's name, do you call me 'your highness,' man?"

"Because your highness is such a great man," replied I, with pleasant significance.

"Pooh! what does he mean?" said he, turning angrily to some of the officers beside him.

These officers, however, seemed as dense at perceiving the exquisite humour of the joke as he was himself, and shook their heads.

"Your highness," continued I, with grave and emphatic

solemnity, and drawing myself up as well as the tether-
ings of my nether garments would allow me, "I am
deeply grieved if in anything I have done I have given
offence, but I pray you to believe that I have always felt
the most benevolent wishes and the best intentions
towards the people of this country. When I knew them
to be hard pressed by the Turks, I flew *vi et armis* to
their rescue, and when again I beheld my brethren in
arms suffering the pangs of hunger, I, at great personal
risk and inconvenience, slew a pig and provided them
with food."

"Saints preserve us!" exclaimed Horvatovitch, banging
the table with his fist with angry impatience, "what is
the man chattering about?"

"This is all very fine, sir," said another officer, "but
be good enough to keep to the point."

I was a little surprised at the general's discourteous
interruption, but replied,

"That is the point, sir."

"Do you mean to tell me," cried the general, "that
you think it right to disobey orders in the teeth of the
enemy, and kill another man's cattle?"

"Your highness will pardon me," replied I, politely,
"if I have failed to regard the matter from the same
elevated point of view as yourself." I then went on to
say that I had never heard of the order, and that I did
not know that the pig was any one's property, it looked
to me like a young wild boar. This statement was
received with a loud and rude burst of laughter.

I drew myself up to my full height, and looking defiantly round, was about to launch forth into an impassioned and eloquent attack on my ill-bred persecutors, when to my utter and irretrievable confusion the strain caused by my upright position proved too much for the wretched button that supported my pantaloons, and it gave way, and they immediately became so uncomfortably loose that I required all my wits to keep them together.

Fortunately for me, Counts Réné and Tiesenhausen came to my aid at the critical moment, and bore witness in very flattering terms to my character and capacity as a medical officer. Their remarks were vehemently seconded and applauded by Savrimovitch, Baron Kleist, Prince Obolenski, and other Russians present, and ultimately the general let me off with a slight reprimand and a recommendation to restrict my abilities for the future to the slaughtering of Turks instead of Servian swine.

On leaving his highness's presence I was escorted to my quarters by a large party of friends, who overwhelmed me with kind and enthusiastic congratulations, and the evening was spent in uproarious festivity.

We did not separate until a vast quantity of weak wine, weaker tea, and still weaker coffee had been consumed, and the hands of our watches indicated the near approach of midnight.

CHAPTER XVIII.

WHEN our party had broken up, Alexis Savrimo-vitch came up to me and said, "There is mischief in the wind, Alfred; we shall have a battle to-morrow. Just after your trial was over an orderly galloped up to Horvatovitch with despatches from General Tchernaieff, and immediately afterwards there was a grand hurrying and scurrying about of the commanding officers!"

"I hope we shall go under fire together!" said I.

"Well spoken, dear friend," replied Alexis, pressing my hand. "If my duties as aide-de-camp do not call me elsewhere, it will be as you say."

For a moment he was silent, then turning to me again, he said in a low voice,—

"Let us say a prayer together, Alfred. I have a strong presentiment that to-morrow will be a fatal day for me, and I would ask the Almighty to enable me to do my duty well and bravely as a good Russian should."

"If it is a fatal day for you, it shall also be fatal for me," I replied, speaking with real emotion; "but I cannot believe that either of us will fall yet—indeed, I feel convinced that we shall both be spared to lead good and useful lives."

"Maybe I am wrong," said Alexis, gravely, "but something tells me to prepare for death."

We then knelt down, and each in turn offered up a short petition to Heaven to watch over and protect us throughout the coming day, and to enable us to die, if need be, as brave Christian soldiers should. Then, as the night was rather chilly, for there was an east wind blowing, we stirred up the fire, threw a few more logs on it, and lay down in convenient proximity, to share the one waterproof we possessed between us. We endeavoured to go to sleep. Alexis, however, was restless and uneasy, and could not settle down. A few minutes after we had wished each other *bon repos* he gave so violent a start that he roused me immediately. I saw that he was sitting up, and staring, with an expression of intense alarm, at some object on my right. Following the direction of his eyes, I was just in time to see what looked like a black dog scurry away into the darkness with a dismal howl.

"The omen! the harbinger of death!" exclaimed Alexis in an awestruck tone.

"Nonsense, Alexis!" said I; "it is simply a starving black cur that has been attracted by the smell of our supper."

Savrimovitch shook his head gloomily. In a second or two he said, "I tell you, Alfred, I believe that to be a supernatural appearance, to warn me of my death. Such an apparition has always been seen before a Savrimovitch dies, and I am the only surviving son of an only son ; but," continued he, resolutely setting his teeth together, "if the arch-fiend himself were to appear and roar my doom in my ears, he should not hinder me from doing my duty to-morrow ! What do you think," said he, rising to his feet and stretching himself, "of a cigarette and a cup of coffee? I sha'n't sleep at all to-night ! "

"With all my heart," said I, rising too.

Now, though I do not consider myself to be at all superstitious, and have no faith in ghost stories, yet the air of conviction with which Alexis spoke, the darkness of the night, and the silence around us, broken only by the moaning of the east wind among the trees, awed me, and I shivered with fear.

However, cigarettes and coffee soon dispersed these uncomfortable sensations, and in a few minutes we were chatting pleasantly together. Then we carefully inspected the condition of our weapons, oiled the locks of our revolvers, and tried the edges of our blades.

After this I became terribly weary, and gradually and unconsciously dropped off to sleep. I know that I intended to keep awake the rest of the night, and shall regret to my dying day that I failed in my endeavour. That was our last evening together! Savrimovitch's forebodings of the coming day were, alas! only too thoroughly realized.

When I had been asleep I daresay about a couple

of hours, I was roused by someone shaking me and saying,—

"Levez-vous, monsieur, nous allons attaquer les Turcs!"

I sat up immediately, and rubbing my eyes, looked around. It was still quite dark, but by the flickering firelight I could perceive that the whole camp was astir. Savrimovitch was lying beside me, fairly tired out at last like myself, so I awoke him. He sprang to his feet in a second, all life and activity, without a trace of the anxiety and apprehensions which he had displayed on the previous evening on his handsome face.

As it was the intention of Horvatovitch, if possible, to surprise the Turks, strict silence was kept in the camp. No bugles were sounded; no talking was allowed in the ranks. Even the officers spoke to one another in an undertone. To me the sight of so many hundreds of armed men, assembling noiselessly together in the cold, dark morning to do battle for their country, was deeply impressive.

Just before marching, the commanding officer of each battalion read out a short and pithy speech from Colonel Medvedovski.

He trusted the soldiers would do their duty that day in a manner worthy of their country and the great Sclav race.

"The first man," we heard, "that lays his hand on a Turkish cannon shall receive forty ducats reward, and

the cross of the Takovo; but the coward and run-
away is hereby sentenced to death." I have omitted
to state that on going to the place where I had left my
rifle on the preceding evening, I found, to my unspeakable dismay, that it had disappeared! Some
patriotic scamp, who had damaged or lost his own,
had appropriated it.

Whilst I was searching for it the order came to
march; seeing, therefore, a rifle that apparently had no
owner lying on the ground, I snatched it up and took
my place beside Baron Kleist and Mouravioff. Alexis
Savrimovitch was close by, mounted on a magnificent
bay charger, and right noble he looked as he reined
in and checked the ardour of the spirited creature.

Whilst the other battalions were moving off, and we
were waiting our turn to follow, he suddenly beckoned
me to him, and putting his arm round my neck gave
me a kiss, and slipped the locket I had seen him wear
and a paper with an address on it into my hand, saying,—

"If I fall, beloved friend, send the locket to the
address on the paper. Adieu!" and he rode off into
the gloom.

A minute after we formed fours, and the order was
given to march. Knowing that the Turkish position
was distant only two miles or thereabouts, I expected
that we should very soon have been at them. But
hour after hour we plodded on, until we must have
covered quite fifteen miles.

I afterwards understood that the object of this wide

detour was to make an attack upon the Turks, simultaneously in flank and rear. The road we followed lay across a very hilly and thickly wooded country, indeed, the whole way, we were either climbing hills or descending into valleys, or passing through forests.

Soon after we started day began to break, and the sunrise that followed was a superb and gorgeous spectacle. The whole eastern sky was a sea of crimson and gold, in which floated a number of island-like cloudlets of the most lovely tints. The tops and ridges of the mountains were capped and streaked with radiant light, and the foliage, on which sparkled myriads of diamond-like dewdrops, looked so temptingly fresh and beautiful that my heart thrilled with delight as I gazed on the enchanting scene. As we surmounted the crest of a hill, I observed with satisfaction that we formed part of a very large force. As far as the eye could reach in front and rear, the sun glittered on the bayonets of our column as it wound its way right athwart the landscape.

About this time it occurred to me to look at my rifle, which was a Peabody. To my great disgust I found that the lever which jerks open the breech was broken. The weapon was consequently useless, so I threw it into a tumbril and trudged along, armed only with my cutlass, revolver, and surgical instruments. The cutlass rather impeded my movements by flapping against my legs, so I unhooked it from my belt, tucked it under my arm, and got on much better.

Suddenly, soon after sunrise, we heard a rattling musketry fire far away on our left.

"Bravo!" exclaimed Baron Kleist, "there goes Tchernaieff! He's tackling the Turks in front, and we are to take them on the rear, and smash them up entirely!"

"Do you think we shall beat them easily?" asked I.

"Bah, I should think so!" said Bernadski, who happened to be close by; "it will be a walk over for us. They'll run like rabbits!"

"They won't show much fight then," said I, rather disappointed.

"They'll be massacred if they do," replied he. "We shall beat them as easily as we used to beat the Turcomans in Asia; they are all the same lot."

Meanwhile the sound of the firing increased until it swelled into a roar as rapid and incessant as the rolling of kettledrums, and the thunder of artillery now added to the din as gun after gun boomed in quick succession. The field of action was completely hidden from our view by a range of hills, but above these thick clouds of white smoke began to rise.

"How many men do you suppose are engaged now?" I asked.

"About 60,000" replied Von Kleist. "Tchernaieff has 30,000 and the Turks as many, and they are pounding away at one another with about 120 cannon!"

"The Turks are not running away yet!" said I, hopefully, because I still longed to see a little fighting.

"No, but they will directly," replied Bernadski.

" They are firing as hard as they can to keep their spirits up, always a last resource of bad troops. By St. Michael, we'll make mincemeat of them if they have not bolted by the time we arrive ! "

" And how many of us may there be ? " I asked.

" About 20,000 and 40 guns."

" By Jove, it won't be a bad battle ! " I exclaimed enthusiastically, as I thought with pride of the yarns I would spin to my friends at the hospital and my comrades in the 37th Middlesex.

For quite two hours after the firing had begun we continued marching steadily in a line, parallel with the range of hills which shielded us from the battle. The column then turned rather sharply to the left and entered a thick forest.

By this time some of the Servians showed signs of getting fagged, and began to lag behind ; and though I was fresh enough myself, still the boots I was wearing, those Mihailoff gave me, galled my ankles, and I stopped once or twice to ease them.

" Hulloh, Mr. Englishman ! " shouted a young Russian, seeing me do this, " tired already ! You Britons knock up very easily ! "

" I am no more tired than you are," retorted I, indignantly ; and to show him that I meant what I said, I leapt over the trunk of a fallen tree that lay a little on the side of the path ; " I'll bet you half a ducat that you won't do that, my boy ! "

The young Muscovite accepted the wager. He was

both taller and more powerfully built than I, but much less nimble, and in attempting the leap, he caught his heel against the bark of the tree and fell heavily, whereat I chuckled and offered to pick him up, with many expressions of sympathy, which he received rather petulantly.

The forest extended up the slope of a range of heights, and marching became fatiguing and difficult. About half-way up we passed large masses of Servian troops drawn up beside the road. These men greeted us with loud hurrahs, to which our brigade responded with equal enthusiasm. I then ascertained that, being considered desperate dogs and fighting fellows, I presume because of the number of Russians amongst us, we were to have the honour of commencing the attack. We were now approaching the scene of action. The roar of musketry became louder and louder, and the thunder of artillery sounded nearer every minute. Towards the crest of the heights the forest thinned considerably, but there were still sufficient trees to afford us cover. The top of the hill was a plateau of irregular shape and considerable extent, on a portion of which, about five hundred yards distant, and separated from us by an indentation or ravine shaped like a *cul-de-sac*, heavy firing was going on. That was part of the Turkish position we were to storm.

Preparatory to making the attack, the officers drew their swords and moved up and down the ranks, shouting, " Forward ! steady ! " I drew my cutlass, too, and lopping down a small branch from an oak, stuck a spray of the leaves in my cap. This little action brought a

12

loud cheer from the Servians who witnessed it, for the oak is their favourite emblem, and I had unconsciously paid them a compliment.

To the front, half-hidden by the trees, were eight or ten pieces of Servian artillery. It must have been terribly hard work to get them into that position, but there they were, with gunners standing beside them, ready at the word of command to send a volley of shells at the enemy.

Meanwhile the whole brigade slowly advanced. Several companies were thrown out to line the crest of the heights, and supplement the artillery fire with their musketry.

By this time it was about half-past ten, and intensely warm.

I noticed several of the timid ones steal out of the ranks, and make off into the forest. Some were caught and brought back, but the majority seemed to make good their escape. Suddenly a horseman, in whom I recognised Savrimovitch, galloped by, and checking his foaming steed for a moment, saluted and said some words to our brigadier, and then dashed off towards the artillery.

Then sheets of flame and vast clouds of smoke burst forth from the guns, as with a crash like thunder a storm of shells was hurled at the Turks. The riflemen let fly a rattling volley, and then kept up a heavy and continuous fire, loading and discharging their pieces as fast as they could. Our drums and bugles now sounded the *pas de*

SERVIANS AND RUSSIANS ATTACKING THE TURKS.

To face p. 186.]

charge. The standard borne by a gallant young Russian named Linden was raised aloft, and the Medvedovski Brigade, in *échelon* formation, dashed forwards at the double, the officers brandishing their bright sabres and waving their caps, and the men hurrahing like mad. We could see the Turks training round their guns to bear on us, and hurrying up bodies of infantry, whilst an ominous glittering of steel was observable amid the bushes in front. For a minute or two they did not fire a shot. The head of our column advanced two or three hundred yards across the intervening portion of the plateau without suffering a single casualty.

Then a Turkish bugle rang out loud and clear, and immediately after the enemy's position was blotted out by puffs and wreaths and films of smoke; shells screamed through the air, and flamed and exploded about us, and a hail of bullets tore through our ranks, knocking over scores of gallant fellows, and dealing death and wounds broadcast. So deadly was the fire that the front ranks were almost annihilated. Poor young Linden was shot dead, but ere the standard had dropped from his dying hand, the brave Mihailoff seized it and waved it on high. Count Tiesenhausen's horse was killed, and he himself wounded in the thigh. Numbers of other officers whose names I did not know also fell—mortally or desperately wounded. The rain of bullets never slackened, and the column began to waver. At this critical moment my friends, Alexis Savrimovitch, Count Réné, Baron Kleist, Mouravioff, and Bernadski rallied and led them on again, and with loud shouts of "Jivio Serbski" we dashed forward once more.

The nearer we got to the enemy the hotter their fire became. Their missiles kept up an incessant humming, buzzing, and hissing about our heads. Again the men wavered, and this time a number of them, seized with downright panic, fairly turned round and ran away. I must confess to having been considerably scared myself. Like lightning the thought flashed through my brain, "What a fool I am to risk life and limb for men who don't know and don't care anything about me. I'll clear out as quick as I can!" but before I had time to stop myself in my forward rush, Count Réné's words, "You are an Englishman, and we expect great things of you," came to my mind, and with an overwhelming feeling of shame for my cowardly thought, I ran onwards a little faster than before.

The number of mounted officers who were struck down filled me with a great terror for Savrimovitch, and I shouted to him an entreaty to dismount; I think he heard me, for he glanced round. The next moment his cap was pierced by a bullet and swept away, and his horse reared up and sank dead under him.

"I'm all right, friends!" said he, springing to his feet. "See how the Almighty preserves us! Naprez Zastava Slava!"

Scarcely were the words out of his mouth than his sword fell with a jerk from his hand, and uttering a painful exclamation, he straightened himself up for a mcment and reeled backwards. I ran up to him and caught him in my arms just as he was sinking to the ground.

"Good God, Alexis!" said I, in an agony of apprehension, "I hope you are not badly wounded."

"I'm done for, Alfred," said he, faintly. "Oh, my arm! Lay me down, there's a good fellow!"

I complied with his request, and then saw that he had received a bullet wound in the shoulder, from which blood was pouring at a terrific rate, his clothes being already saturated. Believing that the axillary artery in one of its large branches had been divided, I ripped up his clothes and attempted to compress the subclavian with my finger, but, alas! my efforts were too late.

The shadow of a smile flitted across his hueless face, his pale lips moved as if he would have spoken, but no sound issued from them. His eloquent blue eyes became fixed and glazed, and with a faint sigh he fell back dead.

For a moment I was scarcely able to realize the fact that my friend was gone. I hoped and trusted that he had only fainted, and I continued to compress the vessel after his circulation had ceased, and to speak to him when his sense of hearing had for ever fled. But it was impossible long to mistake the awful calm and stillness of death, so strange amid the hideous riot and uproar around, and when at length the sad truth forced its way home to my heart, I was utterly overwhelmed with sorrow. The generous and affectionate—if somewhat wayward—disposition of the dead man had made his friendship very dear to me. Soon my grief, however, gave way to a frantic desire for vengeance. Rising from beside the inanimate body, I got a couple of soldiers to help me to move it a little to the left, where it was less likely to be trampled on by the soldiery who were rushing by.

Then, gripping my cutlass firmly and drawing my revolver, I was on the point of dashing forward at the Turks, when a hail from a familiar but discordant voice brought me up sharp.

"Hilloh, monsieur! What are you going to do?"

The call came from Dr. Yermaylaff Giggleivitch, who at that moment rode up with a staff of surgeons and dressers and some ambulance waggons. "Don't you think there's plenty of work here for you?"

"Doubtless, sir," said I, looking at the wounded and dying lying thickly around. "There is much to do here, but you have many hands to do it; and there is more to be done over there;" and I pointed to the front, where the fight still raged violently.

"You'll be knocked on the head for a certainty, if you go there, and, moreover, you will not be able to do any useful work."

"I'll take my chance," said I; "I have many friends there. Meanwhile, will you give this poor corpse a place in one of your waggons? It's a shame to leave it here."

"He's quite mad!" I heard Dr. Giggleivitch say to one of his staff. "Our waggons, sir, are for the wounded, and not for the dead," continued he. "However, I'll see what we can do. Who is the dead man?" and he walked his horse up to the spot. " Why, 'tis the other madman. Poor fellow! Take him in, Krabervitch and Yermo. I am very sorry for him—poor, poor boy!"

In spite of the bullets which were still falling pretty thickly about, the medical men set to work with a will amongst the sufferers who strewed the roadway, and I ran on and rejoined my brigade, which, well supported by other Servian troops, had succeeded in driving back the Turkish infantry several hundred yards, and establishing themselves in a part of their position.

We were unable, however, to achieve more than this, and even this success was only temporary. From the trees and bushes in front and on our right flank came a constant blaze and crackle of musketry, and a venomous spitting forth of fire and lead, which told heavily on our already sorely smitten forces.

This fire increased in severity every minute, for the Turks, seeing the importance of recapturing the ground they had lost, brought up strong reinforcements.

Suddenly their fire increased tenfold in violence, due to the fact that they had succeeded in beating back Tchernaieff's attack, and could now devote all their attention to us. Our soldiers were ordered to lie down, but in spite of this precaution they continued to suffer heavy losses. Shells came crashing among the trees about us, smashing down branches, ploughing huge chasms in the ground and filling the air with humming fragments of metal, and the rifle bullets kept up a constant and angry buzzing about our heads. The Russian officers exposed themselves to the fire with marvellous heroism, and as a consequence a large proportion of them were struck down, and their fall had a very bad effect upon the men.

Whilst I was doing the best I could for a poor fellow who had been shot through the lungs, and was choking in his own life blood, I noticed a stalwart young Muscovite, the same I had challenged to leap over the trunk of a tree, standing close to me.

"What is the use of making a target of yourself, sir, in that way?" I asked.

"To encourage the men, surely," said he.

"I don't think it can be any encouragement to them to see all their officers killed," replied I. "It will do them much more good to see you lying down and shooting comfortably at the enemy."

"That may do for Englishmen, but does not suit Russians," replied the officer sneeringly. Scarcely were the words out of his mouth when a bullet struck him full in the forehead, and he fell back dead. The Turks now apparently thought us too much demoralized to withstand a bayonet charge. Their fire slackened, and a strong body of their men, bursting from cover, rushed at us with ferocious yells and levelled bayonets.

The word was passed down our line that we were to reserve our fire until they came within thirty paces, and then to let them have it.

Seeing that my patient was dead, and not wishing to be stuck by a Turkish bayonet, I picked up his rifle, and fitting a cartridge into the breech, awaited their approach. On they came, rending the air with loud shouts of " Allah !" and a very determined and formidable-looking set of fellows they were—swarthy, wiry, and muscular, with black hair and fiercely gleaming dark eyes. Nearer and nearer they came, shouting exultantly as they fancied we were afraid to oppose them, whilst our hearts beat high with excitement. At last came the signal to fire, and a deadly hail of lead issued from a thousand rifles, withering their brave ranks and driving them back in wild confusion. Rallied by their officers, however, they came on again, but we had had time to reload, and treated them to another tempest of wounds and death. This time they were past rallying, and ran back to cover. We were wild with exultation, and shouted Hurrah ! again and again; but the Turks are bad to beat, and when they had regained cover, the fire to which we were exposed became terrific. By midday it was evident the Servians would have to retire from the position they had won, but up to this time the men had behaved well. The Turks, however, had been preparing a most disagreeable surprise for us. Hitherto the fighting had been confined entirely to our front and right, and our attention being fully occupied, two Tabors were able to work round to our left, and the rattle of their musketry and the whizzing of their bullets was the first intimation of their presence. This was the turning point of the engagement, for the soldiers now utterly lost heart and fled. Their officers made several brave but useless efforts to lead them to drive back the new-comers, but no ; they had had enough of fighting for one day, and had quite made up their minds to run away.

Some of the officers, hoping to check the rush, shot down a few of the first runaways, but all to no purpose. The troops were completely demoralized : they charged past their officers, in many instances bearing them along with them in their rush, and threw away their rifles, belts, and ammunition pouches—everything, indeed, that hindered their flight. A big Servian ran against me and knocked me head over heels. When I picked myself up, which was not till some seconds afterwards, for the frightened vagabond had sent all the breath out of my body, all that I could see of our men were the backs of the hindmost. A few of the officers who had been charged down like myself were lying here and there on the ground.

Meanwhile the Turks continued to advance, and their bullets were singing about us in a way which was decidedly unpleasant.

"Baron," said I, getting up, "if we stay here any longer the Turks will cut our throats."

"Sacré nom de Dieu !" he hissed through his teeth; "I'll never run away from this *canaille.*"

"You look at it in a wrong light, baron," said I. "We are running after our men, and not away from the Turks. Perhaps we can rally them yet."

"You are right, Mr. Englishman," said he, getting up and beginning to run with me.

"By St. Peter and St. Paul, if ever I catch those pigs of Servians who knocked me down, I'll tan their hides for them!"

"By all means," said I, expecting every minute to feel my back perforated by a bullet; "let's run a little faster!"

The victorious Turks, with characteristic indolence, scarcely pursued our army at all, but contented themselves with sending a lot of shells and bullets after us. Had we been fighting any other disciplined troops, our army might have been annihilated and the campaign ended there and then. However, as far as I am concerned, I am very grateful that they were so apathetic.

It is a very unpleasant thing to face a heavy musketry fire, but it is to my mind far more disagreeable to run away from one. In the first case, your mind is occupied by your duty, your desire to distinguish yourself, and so on, whilst in the second, your sole thought and desire is to avoid being ignominiously snuffed out and extinguished. Each time that I heard the scream of an approaching shell, I fancied that I was bound to be hit, and felt correspondingly uncomfortable, whereas scores of them had passed comparatively unnoticed by me whilst the action was raging.

The sensations I experienced were shared in apparently a greater degree by many other fugitives. Some of them scrambled along on all fours, like so many rabbits, others, every time a shell flew by, threw themselves on the ground, and crawling along a few paces, rose again and continued their flight. One man, an officer, particularly distinguished himself by the agile way in which, as he ran, he threw himself on his hands and feet and sprang up again. I watched this india-rubber warrior's movements for some time, when a shell burst close to where he happened to be, and he vanished from my view; but reaching the spot where the missile had fallen, I beheld a horrible sight. Three or four dead and fearfully wounded men lay around, and close to them, stretched on his back, with his chin pointing to the sky, was the unfortunate officer, in whom, to my great astonishment, I recognised my acquaintance, Colonel Bragg.

Whilst I was looking at him, the colonel heaved a faint sigh and opened his eyes, so I gave him a drink of water, and asked him if he was wounded, for I could see no hurt.

"No, thank God! Doctor, I don't think I'm wounded. Ah! give us a drop more water, so. That's good, but the fact is, I'm infernally sensitive, and have a weak stomach, and when that shell burst and blew a lot of fellows into little bits just by where I was, it upset me, and I fainted."

"Well but, colonel," said I, "you mustn't lie here! The Turks will be here directly, and will cut your head off if they find you."

"For God's sake, then, don't leave me, doctor!"

WOUNDED RUSSIAN SOLDIER.

To face p. 196.]

replied he. "Give me your hand, quick!" and he scrambled to his feet. He still seemed rather faint, so Baron Kleist and I supported him between us, until he was steady enough to take care of himself. Presently we overtook a long and dismal train of wounded men, all doing their best to escape. Some were being supported by friends, some limped along painfully with the aid of their rifles or sabres, whilst others again were crawling on their hands and knees.

A very few were on horseback, and these seemed to be suffering terribly from the movements of the animal. Amongst them, grinning with agony, was the brave Mouravioff. He had been shot in the groin, and was supporting himself as well as he could with his hands on the pommel of his saddle. He gave a smile of recognition as he saw Kleist and myself, and begged for a little water. Then we improvised a very respectable litter for him with four rifles tied together with belts and a couple of overcoats, and lifting him gently from his horse, temporarily dressed his wound, and laid him on our ambulance, greatly to his relief, and made a couple of stout fellows carry him.

But the sight which affected me most was the body of Mihailoff on a stretcher. I thought at first he was dead. His face was a ghastly colour, his right arm was shattered, and he had received a wound in the abdomen. But though hopelessly injured, he was still alive, and seemed in great pain.

To alleviate his sufferings, which were aggravated by

the oscillation of the litter, we gave him some opium, and converting the sheaths of two knives into rough splints, we put his arm up.

He was perfectly conscious, and spoke to Baron Kleist and myself whilst we were dressing his wounds, although every now and then he became very faint. I begged him, through the baron, not to talk, but he said he had something on his mind and must out with it, even though it cost him his life.

"I thank God," said he, speaking in jerks, "that—I have been—able to do my duty to-day—like a good Russian and a brave soldier—oh! gently, doctor, with my arm! So!—so!—a mouthful of water, doctor. Thank you. Until I was wounded I did not—think once—of my beloved wife and my—angel-children—for fear of flinching. Ah, doctor!" he continued with a sob, "I shall—never—never see—them more—and my sweet wife will break her heart with grief."

Tears trickled down the poor fellow's cheeks as he uttered these touching words. His distress moved both the baron and myself deeply. For a few minutes we walked alongside his stretcher in silence. But suddenly there arose a loud cry of "Tcherkess! Tcherkess!" (Circassians), and the name of these blood-thirsty horse-men was now sufficient to strike terror to the hearts of our beaten soldiers. There was a scramble and rush to get away; wounded men were bustled and upset, and, dreadful to relate, the bearers of Mihailoff's stretcher, seized with a sudden panic, dropped their burden and

fled. The poor fellow fell heavily, and lay motionless
on the ground. Horror-struck, I dropped on my knees
beside him, but, alas! the shock proved immediately
fatal. A convulsive tremor shook his frame for a second,
and then he, too, was added to the long list of our
dead.

This alarm, which after all proved a false one, caused
the death of several other wounded men. Some were
trampled to death, others thrown violently to the
ground, and, like Mihailoff, died of the shock; others
who still lived were groaning and crying out piteously
with pain. Close to us, a waggon containing six
wounded soldiers had been upset. The unhappy men
were lying on the roadway, piled helplessly one on top
of the other, until luckily the energetic Dr. Giggleivitch
and some of his assistants appeared on the scene. By
their exertions, seconded by the efforts of a number of
soldiers, heartily ashamed of their poltroonery and
anxious to make amends, the waggon was righted, and
the wounded men replaced in it. Then, as we did not
wish to leave the dead body of our friend to the mercy
of the Turks, we covered it with an overcoat and put it
in the waggon also.

Everything possible to alleviate the terrible suffering
around us was done by the doctor and his staff.

It was as yet barely one in the afternoon, and the
heat was scorching. My water-flask was empty, and I
was extremely thirsty, but my thirst must have been
nothing in comparison with that of the miserable

creatures around me, and the cries of pain were
constantly intermingled with agonized supplications for
"Woda! woda!" (water). Unfortunately we could get
no water, and were powerless to give them a drink. No
rations had been served out to the men before starting,
probably because the commissariat had broken down
again, so that very few of us had eaten anything since the
early morning. I remarked to Von Kleist that I was
hungry as well as thirsty, when a soldier who understood
what I said, saluted and said—

"Vrankovitch, yonder, has some cooked pork." Vrankovitch was not an appetising-looking person, nevertheless the baron and I accosted him and asked him to let
us look at his stock of provisions.

"Certainly, gospodina," replied the man, and tugged
a grimy and very unsavoury-looking piece of flesh from
his trouser's pocket.

There was a "greenery-yallery" appearance about
the morsel that was as good as a meal to me, for it
utterly took away my appetite. The baron, however,
being an old campaigner, was less particular, and went so
far as to sniff at it. The sniff was enough even for him.

"That meat," said he with a horrible grimace, "is
tainted and raw. It smells even worse than it looks."

We continued our weary march beside the wounded
for several miles, unable to get any water, but greatly
refreshed by some sour and half-withered grapes that we
gathered from an abandoned and desolate-looking vineyard. These, with some honey which the soldiers found

in the forest, were all that we could find for the invalids. So welcome were the grapes to me that I ate a large quantity of them and a good deal of honey, an excess of which I soon had cause to repent. An hour or two after I was seized with a frightful attack of cramp in the stomach; and sat down by the wayside in great pain. The baron was engaged with a wounded comrade, and did not observe my seizure, and the rest of the long procession straggled by without taking any notice of me. The pain became so severe that I was quite doubled up and unable to move, and to ease it, I took a couple of pills containing two grains of opium. These relieved me very much, and about an hour after I had swallowed them I was able to rise and begin walking again.

Unfortunately, during this rest my limbs had become very stiff and my feet were extremely painful, so after persevering for a few minutes, I took off poor Mihailoff's boots and tried to walk without them. I daresay I managed to creep along for half a mile in this way, a the cost of innumerable pricks and scratches, some of which were really severe. At last my feet were covered with blood, and in despair I sat down once more with the intention of pulling my boots on again. This, however, was quite impossible, and after two or three useless efforts I gave up the attempt. The fatigue and excitement I had undergone, combined with the effects of the opium, now made me so drowsy, that despite the fear of being captured by the Turks, I fell into a deep and dreamless sleep.

13

I T was between four and five o'clock in the afternoon when I fell asleep, and the sun was blazing overhead with undiminished power. I must have slept many hours, but was so tired that I seemed scarcely to have closed my eyes when I was aroused by a vigorous shaking, and saw that I was surrounded by a party of armed men, some of whom held lighted torches which flared fitfully on the breeze. It was now night, and unable to make out whether my captors were Servians or Turks, I put up my eyeglass to see, a movement which elicited much laughter. Then one of them, who was on horseback, said to me.

"Was machen Sie hier, Herr Englander?"

"Ich schlafe," replied I.

"Yes, I see that," said my interlocutor, "but how come you to lie here by yourself?" Though I understood the question, I could not muster up sufficient German to reply, so I pointed to my swollen blood-stained feet.

"Good," replied the officer, "we'll give you a horse, and take you along with us. Jovo, get off that horse and let the Englishman take your place! Of course, being an Englishman, you ride, sir?"

"Of course," said I, ashamed to acknowledge that I couldn't.

"Very well then, up with you, and we'll move off again!"

I felt that it was incumbent on me to vault lightly and gracefully into the saddle, and although I was horribly stiff and sore, I determined to make the attempt. Putting both hands on the saddle, and mentally saying, "One, two, three, and away!" I sprang upwards, only, alas! to come down again on the same spot. I repeated this manœuvre ineffectually two or three times, and at last, much to my annoyance, was compelled to beg assistance on the plea of my lameness. This was readily and courteously accorded by M. Jovo himself, and with his aid I succeeded in climbing on to the animal's back, and I must confess that I never felt more uncomfortable in my life. There were a number of men looking upon me as a wonderful horseman, and expecting to get a lesson in equitation, whilst it was as much as I could do to keep my seat. Determined not to be upset if I could help it, I shortened the reins and gripped them firmly with both hands, and digging my knees into the creature's ribs, defied him to do his worst; and he did do his worst. He kicked and snorted and reared and curvetted and gallopaded about like a furious four-legged fiend. He charged in and out of the Servian ranks, and sent the men flying in all directions. He shook and jogged and jolted me about until my internals felt like a quivering mass of jelly, but resolved to distinguish myself, I held on tenaciously. He twisted round, jumped and jibbed, and made me sick and giddy, so at last I let go of the reins and seized him by the mane and neck instead, at which, wonderful to relate, he ceased from his evil ways altogether, and remained quiet and tranquil, though trembling in every limb.

My triumph was hailed by the Servians with shouts of laughter and applause.

"You are certainly an extraordinary horseman, Mr. Englishman!" said the officer, smiling.

I bowed as gracefully to the compliment as my fatigue and breathlessness would allow, and replied "that the horse was an extraordinary animal."

"Do all Englishmen ride like that?" asked he, laughing rather more than I could see any occasion for.

"No, sir," replied I, shortly, "there are very few of my countrymen who cannot ride a great deal better than I."

The horse was now evidently on its best behaviour. He walked quietly along beside the soldiers, and I felt quite at my ease, and was able to hold the reins in one hand, plant the other on my hip, just as I believe good horsemen frequently do, and converse at the same time with those about me. After a longish march, throughout which my charger picked his way without the least effort at guidance on my part, up hill and down hill and over some very rough ground, we came in sight of the watch-fires of a large camp, and a few minutes afterwards we halted.

I was taken at once to the headquarters of the com-

I DISPLAY EXTRAORDINARY HORSEMANSHIP, AND ASTONISH THE SERVIANS.

To face p. 204.]

mandant of the brigade, in whom, to my surprise, I recognised that burly warrior, Colonel Philipovitch.

" Or, or, dear boy, dear boy ! I am glad, I am glad to see you ! " exclaimed he, extending his arms and folding me in his embrace, " You are not dead ? You are not kill ? Good, good ! And your stomick ? How goes it ? Wie geht's ? Heh ! "

I assured the worthy colonel, as soon as I had disengaged myself from his smothering hug, that I was not dead, but that the important portion of my framework to which he had done me the honour to allude was in a shockingly empty condition.

The kind-hearted officer gave a groan of sympathy when he noted my haggard looks, and immediately gave orders for food to be prepared. He then made me take a glass of sligievitch, which revived me wonderfully. Then after a cup of Liebig smoking hot, I wrapped myself up in an overcoat which the colonel had left me, and was soon fast asleep.

Early next morning I was disturbed by the crashing report of two pieces of cannon and a rattling fire of musketry. The whole camp was in a state of alarm and uproar. Half-dressed officers were shouting words of command, and men rushing pell-mell hither and thither with arms in their hands. "What's the matter ? " exclaimed I to Lieutenant Jovo, as he hurried past me, buckling on his sword.

" A Turkish night attack," replied he, and disappeared.

I strapped on my cutlass and revolver and ran after

him, but in about five minutes the firing ceased as abruptly as it had begun. Then Colonel Philipovitch trotted up on horseback with his staff.

" Pooh ! " said he, " it's only those wild Montenegrins and Bulgarians. Their camp adjoins ours, and one of their chiefs, Luka Vlahovic, has just died of wounds received yesterday, and this is the way they show their grief ! "

" I am glad it's nothing worse," said I.

" So am I, my boy. If the Turks had come thus far, they would have eaten us up altogether, I think, before we were awake. Good-night, go to sleep again." I took the gallant colonel at his word, and lay me down, and actually slept until one in the afternoon.

When I opened my eyes, the colonel was bending over me, his chubby face illumined by a pleasant smile.

" Ha, ha, ha ! " (the sound seemed to come from the depths of his stomach) ; "you have sleeped well, dear boy ; ho ! ho ! ho ! good, and your poor feet ? How is him ? Ha, ha ! you are fatigue ! I am ver dammed busy ; good Englisches that, eh ? Ha ! ha ! ver dammed busy, he ! he ! he ! wit mine two tausand childers here. Grosser famille is that ? two tausand, eh ? Ha ! ha ! ha ! " (then linking his arm in mine) ; " now shall you come wit me, and we shall have some wine and smoke good tabac, eh ? "

" Thank you very much," I replied, " I'll have a mouthful, and then I must be off to my brigade."

" No, no, no, nein, nein, nein, ne, ne, ne " (gripping

me firmly by the arm), "you must not leave me this day, dear boy ; your feet is bad, your stomick is bad, your face is bad ; pell, very pell. To-morrow, when you shall be strong, you go if you will, but to-day, no, no, no ; " and he shook his head and pursed up his fat lips and stamped his feet and looked altogether a picture of resolute negation.

"But——" began I, thinking of my wounded friends.

"But," interrupted he, speaking slowly and emphatically, "you cannot go this day. So I have spoken. What good ? What for ? When you are ill ! To-morrow you shall have ambulance and good horse and go comfortable, but to-day I will not let you, and if you say, ' Colonel, I kill you dead,' your friend still say, no, no, no ! "

The stout Servian was so resolute that I most unwillingly accepted his hospitality. As soon as he found that he had gained his point he ordered dinner to be served, and introduced me to several of his officers, amongst whom I recognised the leader of the party that caught me napping the evening before.

Lieutenant Jovo, the proprietor of the terrible steed I had so successfully tamed, was there, too. I also had the pleasure of making the acquaintance of a huge Montenegrin chief from the adjoining camp, by name Peko Bolrovitch, who had been invited to share the repast.

" In England," said the colonel, ceasing his attention to his soup for a moment and brandishing his wooden spoon in the air, " you eat rosbif and Sauer Kraut, eh ? "

"We eat roast beef," said I, "but not Sauer Kraut."

"What! you eat not Sauer Kraut in England?" rejoined the colonel, his eyes widely dilated with astonishment.

"No," said I.

"Why then do Englanders say when ver angry, 'Ver damm, rosbif and Sauer Kraut? Ver damm, I boxe your heye?'"

I replied that I could not understand why any Englishman should say that unless he were drunk.

"Oho! the Englander only say rosbif and Sauer Kraut when him's drunk!'"

Our conversation was then interpreted to Jovo and the Montenegrin, who received his communication with ejaculations of interest and surprise.

After dinner the colonel beckoned me aside, and said,—

"M. Wright, I will to talk a few with you, sit you down here comfortable; so—good." Then he proceeded to ask me if I would get a medal for him from the English government when I returned home.

"What good will an English medal do you?"

"England," replied Philipovitch, "is rich, rich, and good credit. I am merchant, and when man shall see my Englischer medal, he shall say, 'Oh, see! Philipovitch has Englischer medal, he ver damm respectable, good credit, and rich."

"But on what plea, colonel, am I to claim a medal for you?"

"You shall say," replied he, screwing up his face and

wrinkling his brows in a very odd way, "that Philipo-vitch is a good, good man, that he is Anglo-phil-English lover, eh ? That he is good to you and to all Englanders, and that when he have the medal, he will be better still, eh ? Will you tell to them that, eh ? "

" My dear friend," said I, resignedly, " my influence just now is not so great with our government as it ought to be, and as I hope it will be some day, still, such as it is, I shall have much pleasure in placing it entirely at your service ; in other words, I can't promise to get you a medal, but I'll try ! "

" Dear boy, dear boy," giving me a grateful hug, " I love you much ; you are good friend ; I love you ! "

We now separated for awhile, the colonel and his officers being occupied with military duties, whilst I attended to the hurts of the wounded. These were mostly of a trivial nature, the more severely wounded having been either forwarded to the hospital at Parat-chin, or left to the tender mercies of the Turks on the battle field.

Later on we assembled again round the camp fire. The evening was dark and stormy ; the wind blew in fitful gusts and drove the smoke and sparks into our faces in a very disagreeable manner. It rained, too, off and on, the whole night. The jovial Colonel Philipovitch was, however, equal to the occasion. He had a wonderful supply of good spirits, both mental and alcoholic, and must have possessed an extensive private commissariat department of his own, for he gave us an excellent supper, which included broth and soup and mutton, and even a piece of the prohibited pork.

Nor did his resources end here. Whenever the conversation flagged and the weather became extra depressing, he would produce a marvellous little wooden cigarette holder, with a whistle at one end of it and puffing out his fat cheeks, blow a shrill and soul-inspiring blast thereon, much to our comfort and joy. He had a little clicking machine, too, that he delighted to conceal in the palm of his hand, and when we heard the click, " Was ist das ?" he would say, putting on an expression of intense surprise, and holding up one finger of the disengaged hand, " Was ist das ? Hear you dat noise ? Where comes him from ? "

We pretended not to know, whereat the gallant colonel's delight knew no bounds, and he would click away harder than ever.

Although my heart was still sore and sad after the terrible events of the preceding day, I could not help being intensely amused and joining in the fun.

And whilst this roystering revelry was at its height, a soldier presented himself to the colonel, and saluting, announced that two Bulgarski officers, Captain Milosch Davorin and Captain Ilianovitch, wished to see him.

"Show them here, by all means, my son," said the colonel.

The soldier departed, and presently returned, accompanied by the mysterious person who had so often puzzled me before, and a slim, graceful young officer, who, in spite of uniform and an apparent roughness of manner, was, I felt convinced, a girl. The soldier's companions were most cordially received by Colonel Philipovitch, and cordially returned his salutations. I should very much have liked to give Captain Milosch Davorin a surreptitious squeeze of the hand, but my self-possession failed me, and I felt and I daresay looked nervous and uncomfortable. The colonel introduced me to them with a wave of the hand and an unctuous emphasis on my nationality as his *English* friend, Dr. Wright. When our eyes met, Captain Davorin's assumed an expression of frigid reserve, and greeted me with a distant and formal salute. Captain Ilianovitch, on the other hand, gave me a jaunty bow and a friendly shake of the hand. I felt both piqued and hurt. This cold treatment added to my discomfiture, and so humiliated me, that I meanly resolved to say something very sharp and severe if an opportunity offered.

Naturally enough, the events of the preceding day were the sole topics of conversation for the first few minutes. Gradually, however, we drifted to other subjects, and at last the longed-for chance came.

Captain Ilianovitch inquired of me in French if I had lately heard how it fared with my comrade at Semendria. I fixed my eyes on the beardless Milosch Davorin, and speaking slowly and emphatically, replied that " quelques uns de mes anciens camarades ne sont que des kamaratz." Now " kamaratz " is Servian for mosquitoes, and surely Milosch Davorin ought to have been cut to the heart by this withering sarcasm! I thought it might bring to mind the happy time when he or she used to crush mosquitoes on my face. But astonishing to relate, he, she, or it, the quasi-captain, showed no outward signs of emotion! Of the others, Captain Ilianovitch alone laughed at the pungent pun! I have no heart to describe the rest of the festivities of that evening, suffice it to say that the so-called Captain Davorin maintained an icy reserve throughout, spoke very little, ate and drank scarcely anything at all, and smoked a cigarette or two so charmingly, that the stern resolve I had almost made never to shake hands with him—that is her—again faded quite out of my mind, and I felt again a weak-minded desire to give her fingers a tender squeeze. He and his friend retired after they had been about an hour with us. I would have given worlds to escort them to their quarters, but my late rebuff had been too discouraging. We separated with another 15° below zero military salute. When the party broke up, I rolled myself up in an overcoat and lay down near the fire, it must be confessed, in a very miserable frame of mind. I felt penitent and angry with myself. The more I thought about it, the more this last-named form of vexation grew upon me. I saw how impossible it was for Marie—for I felt positive it was she—to acknowledge me under the circumstances, and I resolved to comport myself for the future with greater dignity and discretion.

I kept thinking over these things and making numerous noble and notable resolutions until everybody save

the sentries were asleep around me, and all would have
been as still as death but for the sighing of the wind and
an occasional hiss and crackle from the fire. Suddenly
the stillness of the night was broken by a frightful
uproar in the camp of the Bulgarians and Montenegrins.
I could plainly hear the report of firearms, mingled
with shouts, yells, and words of command. At first I
thought it was only some more tomfoolery on the part
of these wild volunteers, but the tumult increased instead
of subsiding quickly and abruptly as on the preceding
evening, whilst the sky was lit up with the crimson and
lurid glare of fire. Others in our camp besides myself
took the alarm. Colonel Philipovitch, grumbling vehemently at being disturbed from his well-earned slumber,
hurried about hither and thither, and shouted out orders
and instructions until he was hoarse. The men quickly
fell to arms, and a battalion was despatched under
Lieutenant Jovo to assist our allies. Being very
anxious and uneasy about Marie, I accompanied this
battalion. The night was dark, but the conflagration
gave so much light that we were able to advance at the
double. As we drew nearer, it became evident that a
furious contest was raging. Bullets, too, began to
whistle and hiss over our heads very disagreeably. A
body of Bashi-Bazouks, taking advantage of the darkness
of the night, had attempted to surprise the Bulgarians
and Montenegrins, and had so far succeeded as to fire
part of their camp. Fortunately for us, however, they
had attacked the Montenegrins first, and these valiant

mountaineers, who slept with their arms in their hands, were wide awake in no time, and made a tremendous defence. When we came up, the leaping and roaring flames, the falling huts, the myriad rifle flashes, the struggling figures, the dark shadows of the trees—all this against the obscure background of the night, formed a striking picture.

Without halting us even for a moment, Lieutenant Jovo ordered us to charge the enemy at the point of the bayonet. We went at them with a lusty cheer; at the same time the Bulgarians made a similar advance on our left. This was too much for the bold Bashi-Bazouks, who had merely contemplated comfortably and luxuriously cutting the throats of our friends as they slept, and were, consequently, unprepared to meet with much resistance. Uttering a loud yell of vexation and disgust, they turned their backs on us and fled. This success amazingly stimulated our courage, which had been of the drooping order since the last sanguinary repulse. We pursued them for a few hundred yards in grand style, hurrahing ourselves hoarse, and firing at our discomfited foemen with immense valour and enthusiasm. Our loss in this gallant charge was one man wounded, a gunshot wound in the leg. The Bulgarians and Montenegrins, however, lost heavily. They had twenty dead, and fifty-seven more or less severely wounded. The enemy lost eighty killed outright, and probably many wounded, who succeeded in escaping. No prisoners were taken. The Montenegrins gave no quarter. Every Bashi-Bazouk who fell into their hands was shot or run through the body and beheaded. The Servians were not allowed to do this, but I saw several Bulgarians bringing back pale and bleeding heads as trophies of their prowess.

After many inquiries, I ascertained, to my intense relief, that Captain Milosch Davorin was unhurt, and had returned to camp with his men. This took a great load off my mind, and I worked away for the rest of the night assisting Dr. Tromboni with the wounded. The doctor was an Italian, and nature had provided him with a very fair bass voice, which he was constantly exercising. He performed all his operations to a deep purring accompaniment, and when he did anything particularly neatly in the way of cutting a flap and so on, he would break out into a thunderous series of "Tra! la! la! Ho! ho! ho's!" and, "Bravissimo!" etc. As I can ill bear a noise when operating, I asked him once or twice if he would be kind enough to restrain his musical ardour for a few moments. My request, which was very mildly put, and was by no means intended to be offensive, annoyed the doctor very much, and though he acceded to it, it was with a very ill grace, and we worked much less harmoniously together for the rest of the night.

At 10 A.M., while we were still engaged with our patients, a body of troops, with whom were some surgeons and dressers, marched into camp. The latter immediately came to our assistance, and one of them presented a despatch to Dr. Tromboni from Baron Von Tummy, acquainting him of his appointment as surgeon of the hospital at Uschitza, and requesting him to proceed to his post at once. The officer commanding the troops, an old acquaintance of mine, Nicolai Nicolaitch by name, was quite overwhelmed with astonishment at seeing me. I learned from him that it was generally believed at head-quarters that I had either been killed or made prisoner. After heartily congratulating me on my escape, he informed me that a package of letters and telegrams addressed to me lay at the headquarter's post-office. On hearing this news, I determined to return to my brigade imme-diately. On my way to Colonel Philipovitch, I saw Captain Milosch Davorin at a considerable distance, riding towards the left of the Bulgarian camp. I made a profound salute, which, to my delight, was promptly and gracefully returned. Colonel Philipovitch was break-fasting when I reached his quarters. He was kind enough to express much regret at hearing of my intended departure. Whilst I was speaking to him Tromboni came in with his despatch in his hand, so we agreed to go together.

"But," said the colonel, addressing himself to me, "the Herr Dr. Tromboni have so good a horse, and you, you have no horse. How can you then go together? What will you make?" This sensible question was rather a poser, and whilst I was cudgelling my brains to think "what I would make," the colonel mysteriously added, "I will tell you what you shall make, my good *English* friend. I have two horse, I want them not. They are not beautiful, no, no, but good, yes, yes. Now I will to give my friend a horse, and when you shall be back in England, you shall tell to the government, and shall say, ' My good Servian friend, Colonel Toma Philipovitch, when I have no horse and will ride, give me a horse. He ver dammed good man, and friend to England,' and they shall, I think, ver like give English medal for me, eh ? What think you ? "

"I'm afraid, colonel," replied I, "that our government would scarcely bestow a medal on you for giving me a horse."

" Oh ! but," exclaimed he, eagerly, " you shall say also that I am very, most good indeed, to all English peoples, and that I loves him, eh ? "

I shook my head doubtfully; whereupon a look of the most bitter disappointment came into his face. Suddenly —happy thought !—I recollected an old English Crimean war medal that had somehow come into my possession.

"Colonel," said I, " I can promise you an English government medal, but——" In a moment, before I could get another word out, he had folded me in his arms and was hugging me in a murderously rib-crushing and suffocating fashion.

" Confound it ! " gasped I, wriggling out of his grasp, " let me finish what I have to say."

" Yes, yes, da, da, da—ya—mein frend, das medal ; is it golden medal or silber ? "

" It is silver," replied I.

" Silber, good ! " said he, reflectively ; "silber is very good ! "

" But," said I, " it will not have your name upon it."

" Nichts ! gar nichts. I care not for that, nothing,"
he rejoined.

" All right," said I, adroitly slipping aside, and thereby
narrowly escaping another overwhelming embrace, " you
shall have the medal ! "

The colonel then ordered a soldier to bring the not
" beautiful but good " horse.

The man presently returned, leading by the bridle the
very weediest and seediest, scraggiest and raggedest
apology for a horse I ever saw. It was a four-legged
phantom, a perambulating mass of skin and bone. So
lean was it, that I don't believe a London cat's-meat
man would have given half-a-crown for the whole carcase,
and I doubt if his flesh would have furnished more than
a single meal to a hungry cur. I had seen bad horses
before in Servia and elsewhere, but never, never aught
like this.

As the fearful and wonderful creature stalked by, there
was something so ludicrous in his appearance that I burst
into a fit of laughter.

" Ha ! ha ! " laughed the colonel sympathetically,
" you loaf because he have no meat on his bones, ha !
ha ! I too will loaf—ha ! ha ! ha ! " Then he told the
man to mount and show me its paces. I fully expected
to see the skeleton framework collapse under the man's
weight, but to my astonishment the charger began to
amble easily along in a spectral and dignified manner.

" Well," thought I, " if he'll bear that man's weight,

COLONEL PHILIPOVITCH'S HANDSOME PRESENT.

To face p. 218.]

twelve stone if it's a pound, he'll carry my ten stone without difficulty."

"Dear boy," said the colonel, "that good horse I gif him to you; take him, so, so."

However inferior the condition of the horse might be, I hesitated to accept it as a gift from a comparative stranger, but the colonel was so terribly hurt and offended when I ventured to offer him money for it, that I swallowed my scruples, and forebore to press the point. One thing impressed me favourably about the horse; he did not seem to have a spark of friskiness or vice in his nature, and consequently would not be very difficult to manage. About midday we took an affectionate leave of the hospitable Philipovitch and his officers, and mounting our respective steeds (this, thanks to my late equestrian experience, I managed without mishap), we departed.

Dr. Tromboni had not forgiven my inadequate appreciation of his vocal powers; he was cold and uncommunicative. I was sorry to have offended him, but did not at all regret that his taciturnity enabled me to devote all my attention to my beast.

We went along at an uncomfortable bone-shaking jog trot. I kept a careful look out ahead, and held myself in readiness for such a dreadful contingency as an upset, or an attempt on the part of my charger to bolt, but gradually became less and less apprehensive, and ere I had been an hour on horseback felt tolerably at ease.

My companion was the first of us to come to grief.

Some portion of his saddle gear—I don't know the name of it—gave way, and, to my surprise and amusement, the saddle slipped round the horse's side, the artistic Tromboni slipped round with it, and came a tremendous cropper on the ground. He disappeared in such a comical manner, and threw me into such convulsions of laughter, that I had great difficulty in preserving my own seat. Seeing, however, that the luckless Italian did not attempt to rise, I began to fear he had injured himself severely, and rapidly dismounting, I hastened to his assistance. Fortunately, he was more mortified and angry than hurt, and surlily declining my aid, he got up and put his saddle to rights, and then, without saying a word to me, re-mounted his horse and rode swiftly away. It was my turn to feel mortified and angry now. However, as I did not wish to be left in that out-of-the-way spot all by my-self, I bottled up my indignation, and calling to my steed, which was quietly grazing a few paces away, I prepared to mount and follow the irate Italian.

I called, I say, to my horse, but, to my surprise and dismay, the confounded creature, in place of winnying gratefully and trotting up to me, gave a snort, and shambled further off. Dr. Tromboni was rapidly dis-appearing from view, and I did not know an inch of the way. I hastened after Philipovitch's perverse present, calling coaxingly to him, and trying to beguile him into obedience by such blandishments as handfuls of hay and clover, but to no purpose. The aggravating animal allowed me to come almost within arm's length of him and just as I was beginning to think that I had caught him, he would whisk round, and kicking up his skinny hind legs in a clumsy and impudent fashion, trot to a considerable distance, and then contemplate me with dilated nostrils, and legs wide apart, as much as to say, " I'm not such a fool as I look ! "

This disgusting performance was repeated time after time, with the same ill success on my part, and the same insulting kick-up on the part of the animal as he trotted triumphantly away, until I lost patience, and picking up a stone, I hurled it at him with all my force, yelling as I did so, " Pah ! take that, you accursed creature, and go to Jericho, or anywhere else you please ! Yah ! Booh ! "

The stone, to my great satisfaction, hit him on his hind quarters, and made him cut his capers in quite another spirit, and then gallop off.

This prompt and summary vindication of my wounded dignity warmed and encouraged my drooping spirits, and I prepared to pursue my journey on foot. But here I was in a difficulty. I did not know the way, and a turn in the wrong direction would as likely as not conduct me straight into the arms of those gentle cutthroats—the Bashi-Bazouks. Of course, Dr. Tromboni had long been out of sight, but while I was chasing my horse, I had been able to follow him a considerable distance with my eyes, and struck out accordingly in the direction he had taken. The country through which I was passing reminded me somewhat of the Banstead downs in Surrey, as they were eighteen years ago—a desolate stretch of furze-covered, undulating ground. The horizon on one side was bound by a far-off range of hills, which looked blue and purple in the distance; on the other, by a gloomy forest. After walking for three or four miles, the road branched off right and left, and this brought me to a standstill. Not knowing what else to do, and feeling tired, I sat down for a while and refreshed myself, both mentally and physically, by taking a pull at my flask and munching a biscuit.

Whilst I was thus engaged, a waggon filled with wounded men drove up. I stopped it, and explaining that I wished to go to the Medvedovski encampment, asked the driver to give me a lift. He, a surly fellow, shook his head, and saying "Deligrad," whipped up his horses, and drove away along the road to the left. I was very indignant at this discourteous treatment, but, at the same time, it was something to have found out which road led to Deligrad. So girding up my loins, I plodded on. Presently the sound of wheels was heard again. Looking round, I beheld a light waggon coming along at a rapid pace. There were two men in it.

"These men," said I to myself, "can't pretend they haven't room enough for me."

I stepped out into the roadway and motioned to them to stop. They pulled up at once, but, to my surprise and alarm, one of the men presented a revolver at me, and the other a carbine. "Hulloh!" said I, "what are you up to? I'm a friend—Ingleski bolnitcho—English doctor." The two men whispered together for a moment, and I then recognised one of them as Pauloff, my antagonist in the bedroom at Paratchin. The other was a burly Servian, ill-featured enough, but lamb-like in comparison with Pauloff. They signed to me to climb into the cart if I liked.

Under any other circumstances I should have hesitated to travel in such queer company, but I did not think twice of the matter then, and in a moment I was beside them in the waggon. It would have been better for me if I had been less confiding. In the cart there was a stone bottle containing raki, upon which both of the men bestowed more attention than was good for them.

Presently we came in sight of some cottages, which, unlike any I had hitherto seen in those parts, appeared to be inhabited. My companions asked several questions about the route of a meagre little peasant, whose answers I did not understand, and having bought some more raki, Pauloff resumed the reins, and we drove off again. Shortly after sunset, which was gloriously beautiful, and as the bright glow was fading from the western sky, we came to a deserted wooden hut by the wayside. It was a weird and desolate-looking spot, and, as I entered the cottage, a vague feeling of distrust and suspicion of my companions came over me. I determined to keep a sharp look-out, and furtively put my hand to my belt to see that my cutlass was all right and loose in its sheath. The conduct of the two men, which had hitherto been very surly, now, however, changed wonderfully. The Russian became roughly civil, the Servian almost abjectly servile. They made a fire of sticks and dry brushwood, pressed me to take wine with them, and offered me the most comfortable corner. After supper they rolled themselves up in their coats, and, to all appearance, fell fast asleep. I concluded that I had wronged them by my suspicions, and fell asleep, too.

I was dreaming deliciously of home and of Marie, to whom I fancied I was showing the beauties of Box Hill and of Dorking, when the delightful vision was roughly dispelled by an iron grasp on my throat. I awoke with a gasp, and found myself in the grip of the hideous Pauloff. The fellow's eyes gleamed with deadly ferocity, in his teeth he held a long knife, and with his disengaged hand he ransacked my pockets. Beside me knelt the Servian, who had possessed himself of my revolver, and looked almost as truculent as the Russian. I attempted to remonstrate, whereat Pauloff gave me a most painful prick in the throat with his knife, and, passing his hand significantly across his neck, gave me to understand that he would do for me if I attempted to move or speak. The other villain, who evidently took his cue from Pauloff, thrust the cold muzzle of his revolver against my temple. I was indeed utterly in their power.

The Servian then produced a stout cord, and began to tie me hand and foot in a most elaborate manner. When I first saw the cord I feared they were about to strangle me, but so eagerly does one cling to life that it was quite a relief to me to find that that was not their immediate object, and that a few minutes' respite was to be allowed

me. Although my case seemed almost hopeless, I did
not utterly despair ; indeed, the terrible danger sharpened
my wits. I had been very fond, as a boy, and when a
student, of frequenting so-called spiritualistic séances and
the entertainments given by the Davenport Brothers, and
Maskelyne and Cooke, and had become quite *au fait* at
the rope trick. The knowledge stood me in good stead
now. By expanding my chest to the utmost, and holding my arms a certain distance from the trunk, and yet
in such a way that my captors had no idea of what I was
up to, the fastenings which seemed tight when applied,
became loose and removable when I contracted my
chest and squeezed my arms to my side. Having made
me, as they fancied, thoroughly secure, they left me
lying on the ground in a corner of the room, and
then sitting down by the fire, they proceeded to help
themselves to wine and food, whilst they leisurely examined the contents of my knapsack. To my anguish
they took therefrom all my handkerchiefs, and the only
shirts and socks I possessed, besides those I was wearing.
They next opened my surgical dressing-case, but contemptuously flung it on one side. They took, however,
a bottle of quinine and a box of pills. I remember
hoping at the time that the latter would punish them,
for they were pretty strong ones—Pil. Gambog. Co.,
B. P. to wit.

Then Pauloff, with a murderous grin on his face,
deliberately began to sharpen and feel the edge of his
knife, and taking out my own watch, which, by the way

he had appropriated, signed to me that in five minutes he was going to give himself the pleasure of cutting my throat. I recollect all this as vividly as if it happened only half an hour ago, instead of more than six years. The hands of the watch pointed to five minutes to one. A horrible feeling of dread came over me as I wondered what the sensation would be like when he plunged the knife into my throat. Still I tried to look as cool and resolute as possible, and even essayed to smile, which so incensed the cruel scoundrel that he gave me a dreadful kick in the side, and stamped on my mouth with his heel.

At length that terrible five minutes came to an end, and as Pauloff approached me and poised his knife in the air to execute his threat, I hurriedly commended my spirit to God.

It was not, however, my destiny to die then. The Servian suddenly made a suggestion to his companion which evidently met with his approbation, for he burst into a loud laugh, and returning his knife to its sheath, made a brief reply and pointed to the door.

The other went out, and shortly returned with his arms filled with fuel, which he threw on the floor, and then left again for more. Pauloff, who seemed to be inspired with a fiendish malice towards me, thrust a stick in the fire, and went through the pantomime of setting the place ablaze.

The spiteful glee which this devilish Russian displayed in his efforts to terrify me, and the satisfaction with

which he gloated over my helplessness and agony,
combined with his ape-like appearance, made him look,
by the lurid light of the fire, more like an imp of hell
than a man. Meanwhile the Servian brought in fresh
armfuls of brushwood, and Pauloff was busily occupied
in arranging it about the room. Every now and then he
paused in his work and chatted at me in Russian. In
the meantime I was not idle. My eyes followed the men
in all their movements; my limbs were trying to free
themselves from their bonds. The corner of the room
where I lay was rather dark, and I succeeded in effect-
ing a good deal of this without attracting their attention.

When the Servian had brought in sufficient firing to
satisfy himself and his imperious companion, he proceeded, at the bidding of the latter, to harness the horse
to the cart. Presently he announced that this was done.
Pauloff then took a brand from the fire, and flourishing
it in my face, gave me a parting kick, and set light to
the brushwood in two or three places, and rushed out.
A second afterwards, the sound of hoofs and wheels told
me that they had gone. The brushwood, damp from
recent rain, did not burn very readily, but it threw out
dense clouds of stifling smoke. Luckily I had loosed my
hands before they left, and was thus enabled to clear
myself of the rope sufficiently to crawl about. I
attempted to stand up. The air above was already irrespir-
able, and I was obliged to keep my head as low down as
possible. I crept up to my dressing-case, took out one
of the knives, and cut myself clear. Then I snatched up

my knapsack and made a rush for the door. Fortunately it was not fastened, or I must have perished, for the wood was now beginning to crackle and blaze fiercely, and the heat and smoke becoming intolerable. Pushing the door open, with a cry of joy I staggered into the fresh air, and fell to the ground quite exhausted. How delicious the cool night air felt! For some seconds I did not stir, but remained where I lay, drawing into my lungs deep draughts of the pure and balmy atmosphere.

The flames were quickly spreading to every part of the cottage. They soon burst from the window, and seized on the thatched roof. Then I pulled myself together, girded on my knapsack, and set out along the road, which was illuminated for a considerable distance by the conflagration. Every now and then I turned round to look at the blaze, and when I was about half a mile off the roof fell in, a bright column of fire shot up into the air for a moment, and then the glow rapidly subsided and faded away. As I was trudging along with a heart full of gratitude for my preservation, and wondering if I was to meet with any more adventures, I remarked that a rough paling or palisade skirted the road on my left. I was greatly cheered with the hope of approaching a village. The night was pleasant, and the moon shone with great brilliancy, so that I was able to discern objects at a considerable distance. Some way off I noticed something that looked like a gourd or melon stuck on one of the rails of the palisade. It might have been some thirty yards off when it first attracted

my attention, and as I walked slowly up to it I puzzled
my brains in trying to make out what it could possibly
be. Even when I was quite near I could not make it
out. I put my hand upon it, and found, to my horror,
that it was a human head—whether a Turk or a Servian
I could not say. The head was that of a young man,
and his chin and cheeks were stubbly, as if he had been
three or four days without shaving. The palisade ceased
to afford me any comfort after that. I shudderingly
quickened my pace, and felt thankful when I had placed
a considerable interval between myself and the accursed
spot. I walked on for several miles, until at last a
distant glare in the sky told me that I was approaching
an encampment.

Presently I was challenged by a sentry. I was, of
course, unable to give the password; the guard turned
out, and I was taken before the officer on duty, when
I found, to my intense delight, that I was in the Medvedovski camp. I knew the officer well by sight, but not
by name, and he recognised me at once.

"Why, M. Wright," said he, in a tone of some
surprise, "I thought you were dead, but *milles
tonnerres !* you are wounded and ill. Sit down, my dear
sir; here, take this drop of eau-de-vie. We've another
English doctor here now. I'll send for him. Holà !
Guard there !"

A soldier appeared at the entrance of the hut, and was
straightway sent off for the English doctor.

In a minute or two I heard footsteps approaching to

the accompaniment of one of Moody and Sankey's hymns, whistled in a most lugubrious fashion; then the English doctor entered.

Looking up, I saw to my amazement my dear old friend Hiems.

" What, Hiems ! " said I, speaking thickly, for my lips were swollen and my front teeth loose. If I was astonished, Hiems was almost scared out of his wits.

He staggered backwards, and then gasped out,

" Wright ! Good Heavens ! Is it you or your ghost ? I thought—we all thought—you were dead. It's been in print, man ; your death's been in print ! " and he still looked at me doubtfully.

" I am not quite dead yet," replied I, " though I have been next door to it. Come, don't stare at me like that ! Don't you know me, old boy ? "

" Know you ? I should think I did ! Ain't you the darling of my heart ? Bedad, hurrah ! " and he kicked up his heels in a most unprofessional manner.

" And now, my son, let's look at your injuries," suddenly dropping his Hibernicism and assuming a grave tone ; " lips lacerated, two teeth loose, any bones broken ? Hulloh ! what's this ? " (giving me a punch in the ribs which made me wince); " fractured rib, eh ? "

" No," replied I, " I don't think the rib is fractured. I got a nasty kick there a few hours ago, and the bruise is tender ! "

" Hum ! " said he, " draw a long breath—so ; that's

good—ha! You are not so bad as you might be. We'll put you to rights, my chicken, in no time!"

"Hiems," said I, "why these airs of seniority and superiority? You were not wont to call me chicken and sonny?"

"My dear child," said my irrepressible friend, "if you attempt to command me, I'll put you on gruel and slops for a month. I will, by the powers! Recollect that you are my patient. And now, I'll tell you the news," dropping his voice to a whisper and putting his mouth to my ear; "I'm engaged to be married!" Having uttered these portentous words, he stepped back a pace or two and surveyed me from a distance to see what effect the announcement had produced on me.

"I heartily congratulate you, my dear boy. Who is the lady?"

"But I'll tell you all about it to-morrow, as you must be tired, and require rest."

CHAPTER XX.

THE next morning I narrated my adventures to a numerous assemblage of the brigade officers. My story was frequently interrupted by outbursts of indignation against the villain Pauloff, and when I had finished, I was informed that he had been in bad odour for a long time, and had deserted a few days previously.

"He was degraded to the ranks a month ago," said one of my hearers.

"It is a pity he was not shot," said another.

"Shooting is too good for him, the blackguard!" chimed in Hiems. "I'd like to have his head in chancery this minute!"

"We'll catch and hang him yet," said Count Réné. "Parties have been sent out and are searching for him in all directions, and now, doctor, perhaps you had better see the brigadier, who has heard of your arrival. I'll take you to him."

I at once accompanied the count to headquarters, where I was very kindly received by the grim-looking Colonel Medvedovski.

"I am glad to see you, sir," said he, speaking less stiffly than usual. "On what knight errantry have you been lately engaged? Not occupying cottages again in the Turkish lines, eh, or drilling holes in the heads of wounded enemies, or killing young wild boars to supply your suffering comrades with food?" and his fierce little eyes twinkled with merriment as he poked this feeble fun at me. "Take a seat, and let me hear what you have been doing."

Thus invited, I sat down, and told the brigadier everything that had befallen me since the repulse of our grand attack. He listened with quiet attention until I came to the Pauloff episode; when his eyes flashed fire, and striking the table with his clenched fist, he swore a mighty oath that Pauloff should suffer for his crimes. Then congratulating me on my escape, he told me that a bundle of letters awaited me at the camp post-office, and dismissed me. I was curious to see what the bundle of letters, of which I had heard so much, contained, and went straight from head-quarters to the post-office and fetched it.

The first letter I opened had been forwarded to me from the hospital, and was a dun from a tailor, warning me that if a pair of trowsers I had got from him were not paid for by the 1st of August, he would put the matter in his solicitor's hands. It was already September. The next was from one of my brothers in India, telling me that my father was dangerously ill, and had taken it sorely to heart that I had gone on a wild goose chase in Servia instead of pursuing my studies in London. The third was from Messrs. Deville and Impey, solicitors,

15

Chancery Lane, acquainting me with the death of a
distant relative, whom I had not seen since I was a child,
and whose existence I had almost forgotten, and stating
that they had been instructed by the executors to inform
me that the deceased had left me a legacy of £1,000.
Another was a circular from Messrs Pigswash, Gripewater,
and Slush, wine merchants, directing my attention to the
superior quality of their old crusted port at 15s. a dozen.
Then a telegram from a cousin to the effect that he had
just arrived at Liverpool from America, and asking me
to meet him at 11 P.M., the 22nd August, at the Criterion ;
and lastly, a memorandum from a German lottery agent,
asking me to take a one pound ticket in his government
guaranteed lottery, in which every ticket was absolutely
certain to win a prize, varying in value from £5 to
£50,000 !

The bad news from India, the desire to see my cousin,
and the agreeable prospect of having £1,000 of my own
to spend as I pleased, made me resolve to return to
England immediately.

Returning to headquarters, I applied to the brigadier
for leave, which he was kind enough to accord, and
moreover, he introduced me to a Russian officer, Captain
Starvemo, who was wounded in the arm, and about to
return to Belgrade, and suggested that we should go
together.

This arrangement suited us both very well, and it was
agreed that we should start early the next morning. I
was in a state of the utmost impecuniosity, for the

rascally Pauloff had cleared every coin out of my pockets. I was compelled to part with my surgical dressing-case and the few instruments I possessed to raise sufficient money to pay my expenses by the way. The things were eagerly bought up by the Russian surgeons and dressers, and realized the sum of three Napoleons, of which sum I improvidently expended one-third in bestowing a parting collation on Hiems and some of my Russian intimates.

The next morning, having been duly furnished with letters of recommendation to the Commander-in-chief at Deligrad, we started.

My companion, Captain Starvemo, was an officer in the Russian Marines, and as he could speak English uncommonly well, had been presented with a commission in Colonel Bragg's squadron of cavalry, in order that he might assist the latter, who could speak no language but his own. He was over six feet in height and power-fully built, and though imbued with a strong prejudice against England, confined his dislike to the country and its policy, and not to its people. He was very well informed, and exceedingly courteous and agreeable in manner. Like most of the other Russians I had come in contact with, he was full of the idea that sooner or later they would be at war with us, and when that time did come that we should collapse ignominiously.

"And what would make us collapse, captain?" I asked, as we trundled along the road.

"Starvation," replied he.

" And how are you going to starve us ? " I asked again.

" Very easily," said he.   " You get nine-tenths of your bread-stuffs from foreign countries, our cruisers would intercept your grain-ships, and there you are—starved out; can anything be plainer or easier ? "

" I fancy it is easier to talk about intercepting our grain-ships than to do it," said I.   " What do you think our fleet would be doing all the while ? "

" Fighting with ours, or with those of our allies, or reposing harmlessly at the bottom of the sea," replied the captain.

" And who are your allies to be, may I ask ? " said I.

" Either France or Italy, or perhaps both of them, France is our natural ally, and Italy your natural enemy. A little Russian diplomacy would secure them both to us.   The former sees in us a power capable of restoring Alsace and Lorraine to her, the latter sees in you a rival for the supremacy of the Mediterranean Sea.   Both have powerful fleets, either of which, in conjunction with ours, and aided by torpedoes and infernal machines, would prove more than a match for your boasted navy !

" Hem, sir," said I, " it is very easy and pleasant to talk about these things, but I am of opinion that Russia and France and Italy combined would find their programme impossible.   In the first place, I doubt whether the able statesmen at the head of affairs in France and Italy would let themselves be gulled by a 'little Russian diplomacy !'   In the second—and supposing that they did,—we can fight as well as you, and have torpedoes and infernal machines as good, if not better, than yours, and I am convinced that it would be your fleets, and not ours, that after a conflict between us would be found reposing harmlessly at the bottom of the sea."

" I am very glad to hear you express those opinions," said he, handing me a cigarette, " and I hope they are shared by your countrymen ! "

" To the best of my knowledge and belief they are," replied I, gratefully accepting the proffered smoke.

" Then all I can say is, that the overweening confidence of you Englishmen will be a third and most powerful ally to us. War has its chances, and the mightiest, when most assured of success, have before now come to grief. Mark my words. The very next war you undertake with us or any other great power will place the people of London and Liverpool and Glasgow and your other great cities in absolute distress for want of bread. Any other Government than yours, under similar circumstances, would provide public granaries and storehouses, as a necessary precaution, but you English—no, you won't do anything of the kind. Your thick-headed prototype, John Bull, will go on dozing away and enjoying his dream of fancied invincibility and security until he is caught napping, and then it will be too late for him to bestir himself. But here we are at the camp at Deligrad."

We were now challenged by sentries, and our replies and papers being found satisfactory, we were permitted to go to headquarters. Here we had an interview

with Colonel Comaroff, General Tchernaieff's second in
command. This officer, who was assassinated some
months after at Constantinople, informed us that we
should have to stay in camp for the night, and could
proceed as early as we pleased next morning. It was
still early in the evening, so we whiled away the time
by strolling quietly about the camp and inspecting its
defences. These, in consequence of the untoward result
of the recent actions, were being greatly strengthened.
The approach from the Alexinatz side was commanded by heavy artillery brought from Belgrade and
other fortresses ; all trees interfering with the line of
fire had been cut down, dragged into camp, and stripped
of their leaves, and then piled up with their branches
sharpened and pointing outwards, so as to form an
almost impenetrable abattis in parts where such protection was deemed necessary. Winter quarters were
prepared by digging large chambers underground and
providing them with thick thatched roofs.

As we were returning from our survey, we met a troop
of cavalry conducting two prisoners who were seated in a
cart into the camp. Both prisoners were bound hand
and foot, and seemed to have made a desperate resistance :
for round the head of one of them was tied a blood-
stained rag, and the clothes of the other were torn and
muddy. When we were almost abreast of them my eyes
met those of the man whose head was bound up.
The effect was electrical, his jaw fell, and a look of
the wildest terror spread over his face, as he yelled out,

" Der teufel! der teufel!" and dropped to the bottom of the car as if he had been shot.

It was Pauloff's accomplice, the Servian. The other prisoner, who had hitherto sat with his chin sunk on his breast, also looked up, and I at once recognised Pauloff. The miserable man started, turned pale, and trembled visibly when he saw me.

" How now, doctor?" said Starvemo inquisitively; "you seem to know those men, and they evidently recognise you."

" I have good cause to know them," replied I. " Would you mind asking their escort what they are charged with?"

Starvemo put the question to the guard, and was told that they were charged with the robbery and murder of two invalided Russian officers. They were to be tried by drumhead court martial, and would probably be shot. The escort then saluted and trotted on with their charge. " Now, doctor," said my companion, " tell me what you know about those men?"

Having no wish to give evidence against them, I exacted a promise of secrecy from Starvemo, and then told him of my adventure in the hut and of my narrow escape. His indignation and astonishment knew no bounds.

" That accounts then, doctor, for their fright at seeing you! Of course they thought you were burnt. No wonder they took you for the devil! I think you ought to inform Colonel Comaroff of these facts."

I argued that as the men had been caught red-handed

in the perpetration of another crime for which they were certain to be shot, the evidence that I could give was not required.   The captain shook his head in a dissatisfied manner, and said he knew what he would do under the circumstances, but of course I was the master of my own actions.   The next morning we set out again, reached Paratchin without any mishap, and by nightfall were at Yagodina.   Here, for the first time for several weeks, we enjoyed the luxury of sleeping in comfortable beds.   We were up at sunrise, and had breakfasted and were well on our way by eight next morning.

About two hours after we started, Starvemo had a violent shivering fit, and complained of feeling very unwell.   This alarmed me greatly, as I thought it might be due to some pyæmic process in connection with the wound in his arm.   For want of anything better, I had only applied a water-dressing to the wound in the morning, when it appeared to be progressing satisfactorily, but now, I found, on examination, that it presented a dry and inflamed appearance.   Stopping the driver for a few minutes, I dressed the wound again, and made my patient take a big dose of quinine, the only drug I had at hand. Feverish symptoms, however, developed themselves, and by the time we had reached Semendria (5 P.M.) Starvemo was seriously ill   I drove straight up to the Russian hospital, where Doctors Knifem and Cutemoff, the surgeons in charge, took him into their skilful keeping.   They were good enough to ask me to spend the night with them, which I gladly did.   We watched by

Starvemo's bedside in turns that night, and had the satisfaction to notice a slight improvement in his condition next morning.

Before leaving Semendria I called at the Servian hospital, in the hope of seeing Doctors Ibaum and Stephanovitch, but they had left the place a month since. I then paid a visit to the hospital itself, where Baron Von Tummy's energy had effected a wonderful change. The clumsy and ignorant soldiers were replaced by an efficient staff of nurses, the wards were clean and neat, and the air in them sweet and pure. Altogether, it was completely metamorphosed from the filthy, ill-managed place I had known two or three months before.

Hearing that the steamer for Belgrade was to start at ten that morning, I returned at once to the Russian hospital, bade adieu to Captain Starvemo and Doctors Knifem and Cutemoff, and went on board the boat, which left the landing stage a few minutes after.

I now examined my pockets to see how much money was left. To my alarm I discovered that my capital amounted to four dinars (four francs) only. However, I consoled myself by the hope that my friends in London would have sent me a letter of credit to the Poste Restante at Belgrade. Still, it is not an agreeable thing to find oneself reduced to three-and-fourpence in a foreign country. Whilst I was counting my money, an important-looking young man placed himself opposite to me in an imposing attitude, and said with an unmistakable cockney twang—

"I presume you are an Englishman."

"I am, sir," said I.

"I presume you are returning to England," said he.

Again I replied in the affirmative.

"I presume you have no objection to conversing with a fellow-countryman."

"No indeed," replied I, "I am delighted to meet you."

"I presume," said he, "you are a medical man."

"I am a medical student," said I.

"I presume you'll have no objection to taking one of my cards ; " and he tendered me a piece of pasteboard.

I accepted the card, and looking at it, read the following inscription :

"DR. BEAZLEY SMUGGE,

Green Street, Hackney."

"You are a doctor, I see," said I.

Dr. Smugge nodded in a grave and dignified manner.

"You are very young to have passed your examinations," I remarked.

"No, well, well—no ! " said he, stretching out his neck and combing out his beard with his finger.

"You are an M.D., sir, I suppose ? " said I.

"Well, no," said he, "I am not exactly an M.D. yet."

"What degrees have you then, doctor ? " said I.

"Well, I can't exactly say that I have my degrees yet,

but I shall have, very soon. I'm walking a hospital, you know."

" But what does the 'doctor' before your name mean, Mr. Smugge ? " I asked.

" Oh, well," replied he, " that's one of my father's cards. He gave me a lot of them, so I'm quite entitled to use them, ain't I ? "

" No, I don't think you are," replied I, laughing.

" Oh, but when a man's well up, and knows his work thoroughly, as I do," said he, " it doesn't signify. I am going up for my first college as soon as I get back. I presume you won't mind asking me a few questions in physiology ? "

I was a good deal taken aback at this singular request from a stranger, and replied that I was somewhat rusty in my own physiology, but would do the best I could.

Mr. Smugge graciously replied that he would overlook my physiological rustiness ; so I asked him, " What was the normal temperature of the blood in man ? "

" That's scarcely a fair question, sir," said he, shaking his head deprecatingly, " however, I think I can answer it ; 212° Fahrenheit."

This ridiculous reply sent me into a fit of laughter, at which Mr. Smugge became very indignant.

" Mayn't a fellow make a little mistake sometimes without being laughed at ? " said he, testily.

" Certainly," replied I, " and I must apologize for my rudeness. But is not 212° rather high ? "

" Er—well—perhaps it is a little, but not very much,"

replied he. "Wait a bit, I know. It's something with a five added to it; let me see—let me see;" and he scratched his nose in his perplexity. "Ah, never mind! I can't think of the exact figure now, but I know that a fellow can't live with his temperature above 900° Fahrenheit."

Again I burst out laughing, and again my discourtesy excited the ire of Mr. Smugge.

"Er—a fellow needn't laugh, you know. Ask me another question—something straightforward and above-board, you know, not a pottering thing about temperature. If any of the examiners at the college have the cheek—er—to ask me a question about the temperature, I shall say—er—'Oh, go to Bath, and find out!' That's the sort of fellow I am, you know!"

Subduing my inclination to laugh with the greatest difficulty, I complied with Mr. Smugge's request, and asked him another question—viz, "At what rate does the blood travel through the arteries?"

"Er—any fool knows that," replied he; "a deuce of a rate—a mile a minute; but that's enough physiology for one day. I presume you've no objection to changing the subject now, sir."

"None whatever, sir," said I.

"Very well, then; we'll talk about something else. Have you done any first-class operations since you came here?"

"No," answered I.

"I did some," said he, "but the fellows have no

THE IMPORTANT-LOOKING YOUNG MAN WITH A BEARD.

To face p. 244.]

stamina, you know, and did not survive the most trifling operation. I was baulked, too, of one beautiful job by Dr. Sharp. You don't know that fellow Sharp. All the better for you ; he's not a gentleman. What do you think ? I was going to cut off a man's hand for a wound on his little finger, when Sharp had the cheek to remonstrate with me. ' Surely,' said he, ' you are not going to amputate for that ? ' 'Yes, I am,' said I. ' But it's not necessary,' said he. ' Maybe not,' said I, ' but it's a pretty operation.' ' A pretty operation,' said he ; ' why, you confounded blockhead, who the dickens are you ? What qualifications have you got ? I shall allow you to do no such thing.' And the fellow made such a deuced row that I had to drop the operation. Wasn't it disgusting, eh ?"

" One of the most disgusting things I ever heard of," I replied.

" The profession's going to the dogs, that's what I say. There are a lot of fellows in it nowadays who have no fellow-feeling for a fellow. I was very nearly doing for Dr. Sharp, though. I am not a man to be trifled with, sir; my anger is terrible when roused. I kept my eye on Dr. Sharp after that, and if he had gone a little further and called me a fool, I believe I should have challenged him to fight a duel. If ever you should come across him, you may tell him that Beazley Smugge warns him not to cross his path again ! "

As Mr. Smugge spoke these words he folded his arms, knit his brows, and scowled most horribly.

"You surely would not hurt him, Mr. Beazley?" said I.

"Hurt him! Yah!" (an intensely ferocious whispered snarl); "let him look to himself! Let him take care of his back! I would either kick him or bump the back of his head five or six times on the pavement. Hurt him, indeed!" Having thus given vent to his righteous indignation, Mr. Smugge cooled down a bit, and offered me a cracknel biscuit, which I declined with thanks, whereupon he ate it himself, and told me between the mouthfuls that immediately after his arrival at Belgrade he would cross over to Semlin and hurry back to England, to prepare himself for the first College exam. in November.

"I envy you," said I, "the prospect of returning home so speedily. I must stay here until my people send me a remittance,—*i.e.*, for about a fortnight." This remarkable young man bade me adieu at the Belgrade landing-stage, and went his way.

There was no letter of credit for me at the post-office, and not having sufficient money to pay for a telegram, I wrote a letter to my friends to acquaint them with my impecunious condition. Next I looked out for some place where I could stay until the remittance arrived—a work of some difficulty, for my unkempt and tatterdemalion appearance went sorely against me, but I at last succeeded in getting a bedroom at the Alexandra Hotel, near the market-place. However, I was not destined to stay there long. The same evening I had a violent attack of ague, and not being able to get proper attention at the hotel, I applied for admission into the English Ambulance Hospital, where I was immediately received and most kindly treated.

The day after my admission acute dysentery set in, and for three weeks I was confined to my bed.

One day, as I was getting better, some visitors who were being shown through the wards stopped close to my bedside, and began conversing in low tones. I was nearly asleep at the time, but one of the voices aroused me. It was Marie's! She had resumed her proper attire, and was leaning on the arm of a tall, handsome man in the uniform of the Bulgarian legion.

Presently Marie saw me, and coming forward, addressed me in such graceful and sympathetic terms that I quite lost my heart to her again. After speaking to me for a few minutes, she introduced her tall companion to me as her *husband*, Colonel Nicholas Davorin, of the Bulgarian Brigade. This was a terrible shock! For a minute or two I utterly collapsed; my head swam round, and I could hear nothing in my ears but the words—" my husband ! "

When I came to, they had gone.

    *   *   *   *   *   *   *

So great was my disappointment at discovering that Marie was married, that I remember wishing at the time that I might never get better. For one whole day I know that I refused all food, and for a week I resolutely declined taking more than half my allowance. My disgusting constitution, however, survived it all, and three weeks after my last unhappy interview with Marie I was on my way home to England,—not, as I had once fondly hoped, a highly distinguished and happily plighted individual, but a nearly extinguished and completely blighted being.

Once arrived in England, however, the kindly faces and hearty greetings of friends and relatives went far to soothe my wounded susceptibilities, and I once more resumed my place at home and my studies at the hospital, a sadder, but it is to be hoped also, a considerably wiser man.

THE END.

Printed by Hazell, Watson, and Viney, Limited, London and Aylesbury.

Trieste

Trieste Publishing has a massive catalogue of classic book titles. Our aim is to provide readers with the highest quality reproductions of fiction and non-fiction literature that has stood the test of time. The many thousands of books in our collection have been sourced from libraries and private collections around the world.

The titles that Trieste Publishing has chosen to be part of the collection have been scanned to simulate the original. Our readers see the books the same way that their first readers did decades or a hundred or more years ago. Books from that period are often spoiled by imperfections that did not exist in the original. Imperfections could be in the form of blurred text, photographs, or missing pages. It is highly unlikely that this would occur with one of our books. Our extensive quality control ensures that the readers of Trieste Publishing's books will be delighted with their purchase. Our staff has thoroughly reviewed every page of all the books in the collection, repairing, or if necessary, rejecting titles that are not of the highest quality. This process ensures that the reader of one of Trieste Publishing's titles receives a volume that faithfully reproduces the original, and to the maximum degree possible, gives them the experience of owning the original work.

We pride ourselves on not only creating a pathway to an extensive reservoir of books of the finest quality, but also providing value to every one of our readers. Generally, Trieste books are purchased singly - on demand, however they may also be purchased in bulk. Readers interested in bulk purchases are invited to contact us directly to enquire about our tailored bulk rates. Email: customerservice@triestepublishing.com

You May Also Like

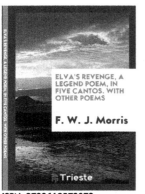

ELva's Revenge, a Legend Poem, in Five Cantos. With Other Poems

F. W. J. Morris

ISBN: 9780649573073
Paperback: 146 pages
Dimensions: 6.14 x 0.31 x 9.21 inches
Language: eng

Longmans' English Classics; Dryden's Palamon and Arcite

William Tenney Brewster

ISBN: 9780649565733
Paperback: 170 pages
Dimensions: 6.14 x 0.36 x 9.21 inches
Language: eng

www.triestepublishing.com

You May Also Like

ISBN: 9780649066155
Paperback: 144 pages
Dimensions: 6.14 x 0.31 x 9.21 inches
Language: eng

Heath's Modern Language Series. Atala

François-René de Chateaubriand & Oscar Kuhns

ISBN: 9780649607242
Paperback: 172 pages
Dimensions: 6.14 x 0.37 x 9.21 inches
Language: eng

Hour by Hour; Or, The Christian's Daily Life

E. A. L.

You May Also Like

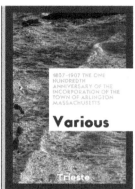

ISBN: 9780649420544
Paperback: 108 pages
Dimensions: 6.14 x 0.22 x 9.21 inches
Language: eng

1807-1907 The One Hundredth Anniversary of the incorporation of the Town of Arlington Massachusetts

Various

ISBN: 9780649194292
Paperback: 44 pages
Dimensions: 6.14 x 0.09 x 9.21 inches
Language: eng

Biennial report of the Board of State Harbor Commissioners, for the two fiscal years commencing July 1, 1890, and ending June 30, 1892

Various

You May Also Like

Biennial report of the Board of State Harbor Commissioners for the two fisca years. Commeneing July 1, 1884, and Ending June 30, 1886

Various

ISBN: 9780649199693
Paperback: 48 pages
Dimensions: 6.14 x 0.10 x 9.21 inches
Language: eng

Biennial report of the Board of state commissioners, for the two fiscal years, commencing July 1, 1890, and ending June 30, 1892

Various

ISBN: 9780649196395
Paperback: 44 pages
Dimensions: 6.14 x 0.09 x 9.21 inches
Language: eng

Find more of our titles on our website. We have a selection of thousands of titles that will interest you. Please visit

www.triestepublishing.com

Lightning Source UK Ltd.
Milton Keynes UK
UKOW06f1109231017

311488UK00006B/1198/P